Business Writing the Modular Way

Business Writing the Modular Way

*How to Research, Organize
& Compose Effective
Memos, Letters, Articles,
Reports, Proposals, Manuals,
Specifications & Books*

Harley Bjelland

amacom

American Management Association

Library of Congress Cataloging-in-Publication Data

Bjelland, Harley.
    Business writing the modular way : how to research, organize &
compose effective memos, letters, articles, reports, proposals,
manuals, specifications & books / Harley Bjelland.
        p. cm.
    Includes bibliographical references and index.
    ISBN 0-8144-5034-2
    1. Business writing. I. Title.
HF5718.3.B5   1991
651.7'4—dc20   91-53049
                                                     CIP

Printing number

10 9 8 7 6 5 4 3 2 1

To the continuing joys of my life,
my five "kids,"
who are all now making it on their own:

Carol

David

Harley II

Darlene

Sandra

Contents

Part II Modular Writing Applications

Acknowledgments

Once again my wife, Dorrie, has been infinitely patient during the long gestation, isolation, and perspiration periods required for this book.

I extend special thanks to Andrea Pedolsky, acquisitions editor at AMACOM Books, who believed in my ideas, helped me along the way, and encouraged me to put my ideas to the test of writing them for all to see. Her editing suggestions were invaluable.

I am grateful to Floyd Ashburn, owner of Compatibility + Plus in Springfield, Oregon, and his right-hand man, Jim Schaffitz. Both combined to elevate my IBM XT clone to a higher plane, a faster-working and more efficient AT. They also rescued me from some possible disasters.

The staffs of the Eugene and Springfield public libraries were most helpful and never seemed to lose their patience when I bombarded them with question after question.

And thank you again, Thor, my computer, who accomplished most of the drudgery aspects of writing, giving me time to think and create.

Introduction

This book is aimed at helping you achieve better written communication. It's difficult to overstate the importance of good communication. Whether it's a memo, a letter, an article, a report, or a proposal, we are often judged by the way we write.

Although there are many modern computer tools at our disposal, programs have computerized only some of the more onerous writing tasks. Modern technology is of no use unless people can write and communicate clearly, accurately, and efficiently—and not even the most modern and sophisticated computer programs can transform poor writing into good. The basic writing steps—creating and planning—have not been solved by computers. This book addresses these fundamental steps; it introduces unique concepts and new techniques that will revolutionize the manner in which you create and compose your written communications.

Part I of *Business Writing the Modular Way* ("The Basics of Modular Writing") has been designed to be read from beginning to end. These chapters form a vital series of sequential activities that show you, step by step, how to accomplish the basic research, organization, and writing for all types of business communications. Part II ("Modular Writing Applications") then covers the specific requirements of the different formats used in business, ranging from a simple memo to a full-length book. The chapters in Part II are self-contained and can be read modularly in any order you please.

To use this book most efficiently, first read this entire Introduction; then scan the Contents for a quick outline of the topics covered. I have used a number of illustrations to help explain how the various writing formats are researched, organized, and written. Thumb through the book, looking over some of the illustrations to see how they expand on and illuminate the text.

Chapter 1 provides a good summary of the topics that will be covered in the book and introduces you to two important new concepts: the Precedent Sort and modular writing. If you now dread writing, these concepts will change your attitude. Adapted from computer programming principles, these revolutionary techniques provide logical methods that simplify many aspects of the writing process. The Precedent Sort and modular writing are unique to me and for the first time are applied in this book to all aspects of business writing.

Chapters 2 through 9 introduce and explain the Precedent Sort and show how it can be used for modular writing. They also discuss the precepts of good writing and how to achieve it and how and where to conduct library and on-line research. Most important, they explain the basic techniques of top-down design used in outlining material and bottom-up writing for composing your prose.

Each chapter in Part II focuses on the specialized formats used in the business and professional worlds: the periodical article, the report, the manual, the proposal, several other special formats, and, finally, the pinnacle of written communication, the book.

When you read through this manual, keep a marking pen nearby and underline or highlight the points you particularly want to remember. This also helps you locate the important points you may want to return to and review later.

This book was written not just to be read, but to be used. Use it well, and you'll soon discover that your written communications will be easier to compose, a delight to write, and easy to understand.

Part I
The Basics of Modular Writing

1
Organization: The Key to Modular Writing

Order and simplification are the first steps toward the mastery of a subject.

—Thomas Mann

Much of business today is transacted in writing, so sooner or later every employee must learn how to put his or her ideas on paper. Personal computers, now the primary tool for creating and often for transmitting most communications, are revolutionizing many aspects of writing. Word processing programs format, display, store for easy recall and editing, and flawlessly print out documents. Complementary programs check spelling at microsecond speeds. On-line thesauruses help you select the optimum words to express your thoughts precisely. Grammar checking programs remind you to heed the myriad proved English rules you once knew but that now lie hidden deep in your subconscious.

In spite of these revolutionary advances in technology, one vital aspect of business writing has been sorely neglected: applying these new techniques to the preliminary writing steps of originating, researching, and organizing the raw material. This book is dedicated to these indispensable steps and introduces two new concepts that are ideal complements to the advanced computer programs that now enhance writing: modular writing and the Precedent Sort.

Over the past few years, computer experts have applied so-called structured programming techniques to create and improve versatile and ingenious word processing programs. They have also developed many other complementary software programs that take much of the drudgery out of writing. What could be more logical than to use these professionally devised techniques to assist and augment business writing?

The Modular Writing Process

Modular writing is a logical procedure by which a writing project—a memo, report, proposal, article, full-length book—is divided into small, easily manageable modules, each with a definite beginning, a middle, and an end. Each module can be independently researched, organized, and written as a small, easy-to-accomplish project. When all the individual modules are completed, they are joined together with appropriate transitions to create a logically organized, smooth-flowing, easy-to-read, and easy-to-understand product.

I developed the concept of modular writing by adapting a number of modern computerized techniques to simplify writing. These techniques include the top-down design and bottom-up writing principles programmers utilize. Computer experts tackle a huge programming project (such as a word processing program) by breaking it down into individual modules or subroutines, each designed to accomplish a unique and complete function. Each module is coded (written) from the bottom up, using the native language of the computer. When all these modules are connected together by transitions under the control of a master program, they form a complete, integrated, compatible, versatile program.

Similarly, modular writing uses structured programming principles to break writing down into a two-phase process:

1. Design a manuscript from the top down (research and outline).
2. Build the manuscript from the bottom up according to the top-down design (write to the outline).

A manuscript, whether it is for an article, a proposal, a manual, or a book, should be designed (planned) from the top down. Begin with an overall concept, an idea, a title, or a purpose, and then research the topic and design down to the lowest level of detail needed. The result of this top-down design is a detailed outline that forms a specific plan to follow in writing the text.

The text, conversely, is built from the bottom up. Begin with words;

build them up into phrases, then sentences, then paragraphs, then modules, etc., following the detailed outline until the material accumulates to form a complete manuscript.

Writing in Any Order

Because of the comprehensive outline that results from top-down design, modular writing permits designing and writing any portion of a manuscript in any order that is optimum for the creator of the manuscript. No longer do you have to write from the beginning, straight through to the end of your manuscript. You can begin where your inspiration leads you, and then design and write your masterpiece in any order that works best for you.

One important point to note is that both top-down design and bottom-up writing are highly iterative processes. It's very difficult for a person with an active mind to focus all energy on one narrow aspect of a topic to the exclusion of all others. Most likely you'll be working on one module and suddenly have an inspiration that fits in a different module. That's where your detailed outline comes in handy. When you get your inspiration, jump to the appropriate point in your outline and make a note. Then return to your original module, and continue where you left off. Later, when you rewrite or review the module you added your sudden inspiration to, you can integrate your new ideas into the outline or text.

Any writing format can be designed top down and written bottom up, but you need a master plan that ties them all together. That plan is the *outline*, the *organization*.

Organization in Writing

The most important quality of good writing is clarity. Your writing is clear when your reader understands its exact meaning on the first reading. Clarity results largely from proper organization of your topics before you start writing. Thus, the most important single key to understanding written communication is *good organization!*

"Order is heaven's first law," wrote Alexander Pope. Our minds demand order, form. Your sentences, your paragraphs, your pages may have all the facts, but their meaning may be murky unless you have used proper order, grouping, subordination, and logical links. Your readers have neither the time, the patience, nor probably the knowledge to invest the effort required to sort these out. Your task as a writer is to make the requisite effort so your readers need to expend only a minimum of energy to read and understand your prose.

Organizing your material is much like taking a random, meaningless jumble of words, such as:

Return		the		Harold
	spreadsheet		to the	hit
long	key			print

and organizing them into a coherent sentence: "Harold hit the Return key to print the long spreadsheet."

You must have a systematic, overall plan of development to carry readers logically from point to point. This plan is the outline, the organization, the ordering of material. The major function of an outline is to break your writing project down into small, manageable modules that will help you achieve this logical progression.

Figure 1-1 is an example of the type of outline that I use. I've outlined a portion of Chapter 1 to illustrate my procedure and to define a module and a submodule. Modules are designated by a single dash (-) and submodules by a double dash (--) and a single indent preceding them. The expansion of the topic under a submodule is designated by a triple dash (---) and a double indent. Note that *no roman numerals are used.* Also note that I don't number outline entries so I won't have to renumber them every time I iterate and rearrange my topics. For outlines, don't worry about capitalization, sentence construction, or punctuation. Your concerns are order, logic, completeness, and clarity.

In addition to the outline illustrated in Figure 1-1, I also accumulated a number of detailed notes, photocopied materials, and so forth that tied directly into and expanded on the topics I planned to cover. I reviewed this supporting material in detail before I wrote the text for this chapter. The writing procedure I use is described in Chapter 9.

A document that is properly researched and organized is already half-written. Yet one of the most difficult tasks, most writers agree, is organizing their work. In a comprehensive survey conducted by Terry C. Smith, over one thousand professionals were asked what bothered them the most about report writing. Leading the list of dozens of complaints, at 28 percent, was "organizing and outlining."*

*"What Bugs Engineers the Most About Report Writing," *Technical Communications* 22: 4 (1976).

Figure 1-1. Outline of portion of Chapter 1 of *Business Writing the Modular Way.*

Chapter 1

- Curse of Roman Numerals *[module]*
-- Painful memories in school *[submodule]*
-- Outlining *after* writing is bad
-- Outlining reins in your writing efforts
--- If you can't outline, you're not sure what you're writing about *[expansion of topic]*
- Modular writing
-- People believe they must start at the beginning
-- Outlines *enhance* creativity
-- Write modules in any sequence
- Stretchable page
-- Word processor insert mode
-- Input outline into WP
-- Stretchability somewhat limited
- Iterating
-- Writing is highly iterative
--- How to capture an idea
-- Outline can be reordered easily in a wp
-- Modular writing for typewriters
- Basic writing steps
-- Outline
-- Write
-- Many skip first step
-- We don't think in a beginning-to-end order
--- Thoughts are random, loosely connected

In another survey, conducted by Blaine McKee with members of the Society for Technical Communication, professionals who earn their livelihood from technical writing, a mere 5 percent claimed they used no outlines for their writing in an article entitled "Do Professional Writers Use an Outline When They Write?" Undoubtedly the inept writing you may have suffered through while struggling with confusing manuals for your home appliances or your assemble-it-yourself purchases were written by this unorganized 5 percent.

The Curse of Roman Numerals

You may still have painful memories of being forced to outline stories, or articles, or even books in your high school or college classes by using roman numerals. Well, this Curse of the Roman Numerals (CRN) is about to be lifted from you. Never again will you have to remember how to count, roman style. In this book, the CRN method has been replaced by a logical, simple, easy-to-use outlining technique that *does not use a single roman numeral!*

It was not only roman numerals that made outlining such a tedious and meaningless chore. Typically your task was to outline someone else's material, *after* it was written. You were supposed to be able to remove the lean flesh from the bones of a skilled, cerebral author's writing and emerge with a perfectly formed skeleton. This is wrong. It's very difficult to try to second-guess authors and attempt to divine how and why they organized their topics in a specific way.

Outlining must be done before writing has begun. Only in this manner can you form the proper skeleton, make sure that all the joints are assembled in the correct order, see that no unneeded joints or limbs are included, and be assured that your fleshed-out material will form an exemplary model of cogent and slender prose.

Another important function that outlining serves is to manage and to supply a rein on your writing efforts. If you maintain that you can't outline your topics, you're admitting that you don't know what you're going to write about. And if you start writing before you know your subject, your writing will be as circuitous and as hazardous as a maze. You must establish what you're going to cover before you begin to write.

It's difficult to overemphasize the importance of a comprehensive outline. A well-prepared outline guides you in the logical, step-by-step development of your topics. It forces you to design your document in detail rather than just let it accumulate randomly as you write. Moreover, it is easier to work with—molding, modifying, developing, reviewing, evaluating, correcting, and rearranging—than it is to wrestle with a written draft of muddled writing.

The big payoff from organizing and outlining your writing comes when you have to create a large document, such as an in-depth article, a research study, a lengthy proposal or report, or a full-length book. Nevertheless, you should also invest the requisite time in organizing short memos and letters that you probably could outline in your head. You gain experience in using these techniques, and memos and letters will be easier to write, more concise and direct, better composed, and easier to understand.

Modular Writing

One of the biggest obstacles in writing is that many people believe they must start at the beginning, write down all the details in sequence, and go all the way straight through to the end. An outline helps eliminate this misconception. Yet some writers, because of bad experiences with outlines in high school and college, fear that outlines stifle creativity. But that is not true, as you will learn from this book.

Instead of stifling creativity, the use of a comprehensive outline actually *enhances* a writer's creativity. When you design and write modularly, it's neither necessary nor desirable to write your document in series. You need not start at the beginning of module 1, design and write all the way, straight through to the end of module 1, then go on to design and write the beginning of module 2 and continue designing and writing one module after another until you reach the last one.

Instead, you can work in any way that is optimum for you and create your material in a random sequence, one module at a time. It's best to research and write the chapter or module or paragraphs that you know the most about, or the one you have the most information or enthusiasm about, first, to achieve a positive start. Then jump to any other module or chapter, researching and writing those portions using the detailed outline as your guide. The outline gives you the confidence that the other modules will be completely covered in turn.

The Stretchable Page

One of the most important capabilities of modern word processing programs is their ability to insert information. It is this function that helps make modular writing so effective. The Insert function lets you add virtually any amount of information to any part of your manuscript. The words already stored in the electronic manuscript simply move back to make room for the new material. This vital insert function gives you what I call a stretchable page.

When I write, I input my outline into my word processor. Then, after I've brainstormed and researched, I add my notes, comments, text, questions, and anything else that is relevant under the appropriate module headings. The page automatically stretches to accommodate the new material without losing any of the information already there. Later, when I write the text for a module, using my outline as my guide, the page stretches to make room for the new material.

When you work with a document that is very long (more than about 100 pages), some of the editing features of the word processing program are considerably slowed down, so break longer manuscripts into individual chapters and store them as separate documents of less than about 30 to 40 pages.

Iterating

There are three keys to effective outlining and easy writing:

1. Iterate.
2. Iterate.
3. Iterate.

The journey between an idea and a completed manuscript is far from being a straight line. Writing is a highly iterative process. When you're brainstorming, researching, or writing a module, you'll often come up with an idea for a topic that belongs in another module. Ideas are often fragile and must be captured immediately, so whip out a 3- by 5-inch note card and record your brainstorm; then file it with your other notes or, if you're using your computer, hit the Return (or Enter) key a couple of times and input a couple of "at" signs (@@ —use that symbol or any other symbol you seldom use) to mark the start of the idea. Then hit the Return key again and immediately input your new idea. When you finish, put a couple of more "at" signs at the end to show where the idea ended and continue where you left off earlier. Your idea is now stored for posterity. When you finish working with that particular module, use the Search function to locate the double "at" signs (@@) and then use the "cut-and-paste" function to transfer the idea to a separate disk file that you can call something like "ideas" and store it there temporarily. Finally, refer to your stored outline to determine where the new idea belongs. Cut and paste that new thought out of your idea file and insert it into the proper spot in your outline. If it's a totally new topic, find the correct place for it and insert it in that part of the outline.

If you write with a typewriter, you can still use this modular procedure. Obtain a large looseleaf notebook (about 2 inches) and insert several dividers, labeling them, one for each module or chapter. Type your outline and place it at the front of the notebook. As you design and then write your modules or chapters, file those pages behind the appropriate divider, using the detailed outline as a guide. Skip around randomly, and write as the writing spirit moves you.

The Basic Writing Steps

There are two basic steps in all writing:

1. Organize your ideas.
2. Write.

Nevertheless, many people skip the first step; they dive right in and start writing. Invariably they end up thrashing about, and finally drowning in a rambling, obtuse, turgid, circumlocutious document that is difficult to write and even more difficult to read and comprehend. Even if all the facts are included and each sentence makes sense, unless the document is arranged in a logical order, it cannot paint the desired picture in the readers' mind.

Good writing seldom, if ever, results from a single-step process. Writing is not the simple process of putting words down on paper or of inputting them into a word processor. Several logical steps must be followed in the proper sequence to create good writing.

Organizing Your Thoughts: A New Technique

Begin by organizing your creative, random thoughts into some logical order that will make sense to your readers before you start to write. This effort will:

- Make your writing easier because it will help you relate and properly emphasize certain modules.
- Provide direction for your writing so it won't wander and so you can compose a smooth-flowing document.
- Help you include all the ideas you want to cover in a logical, unified, and complete sequence.
- Make your writing easier to read and to understand.
- Let you begin by writing any module in your outline.

A good outline is a strong writing skeleton that can be expanded with additional explanations, examples, and proofs to create a well-formed, complete body. If the skeleton is not assembled and fleshed out properly, the body will not operate smoothly but in jerky, disconnected movements.

No doubt the outlining techniques you've used in the past gave you much confusing theory but little logical help with this important task. You've probably wrestled and lost with the inverted pyramid, the suspense formula, how to indent, subordinate, use roman numerals, and so on. But none of these has provided you with a simple, orderly, one-two-three way to organize and assemble your raw material together—until now.

In the early development of computer technology, little order existed among the many methods used to program computers. Different programmers developed their own unique techniques that suited their particular approach. Each programmer wrote computer code, debugged it, revised it, debugged it again and again until the program finally worked, after a fashion. The result was often what was called "spaghetti coding": a computer program that lacked logic, had no particular order, and was as scrambled as a plate of spaghetti.

As software grew in complexity and as more and more money and time were wasted attempting to unravel the spaghetti coding to correct bugs and to make updates, some forward-looking computer programmers decided it was time to impose order on this programming chaos. A major result of these extensive organizing efforts was top-down or structured programming: designing, organizing, and modularizing a program in minute detail before writing the detailed programming codes. As a result of these highly successful efforts, programmers soon learned to live by an important aphorism: "The sooner one starts writing code (without proper organization), the longer it will take to finish the program." The same situation exists in all types of writing. The sooner one sits down and writes without proper organization, the longer it will take to revise and unravel the spaghetti paragraphs and phrases.

Over the past twenty-five years I've devoted considerable time and effort to researching, developing, and testing various methods of organizing writing. One specific technique I considered adapting from computer programming is a sorting technique called the *bubble sort*. After considerable experimentation, I decided this versatile procedure was ideal for organizing a random group of related writing topics into a logical order. I adapted it to a new technique for organizing writing, the *Precedent Sort* (P-Sort). The Precedent Sort shows how to gather randomly generated topics and ideas and construct a properly assembled outline that can form the basis for any type of writing.

Without some logical procedure, it's very difficult to evaluate simultaneously ten to fifty or a hundred randomly created and related modules and notes and decide, by laborious trial and error, the order in which they should be arranged. The Precedent Sort, described in Chapter 3, puts order and logic into the task of outlining. It breaks down a complex organizing task into a series of simple decisions and shows you how to compare modules or topics, one pair at a time, and decide which has precedence, that is, which should be covered first in your document. When you have made all possible comparisons, your organization is complete.

Overcoming the Curse of the Blank Page

Two of the biggest problems facing writers are:

1. What to write first.
2. What to write next.

A blank page can paralyze even the most confident writer. Even when you bravely break through this initial barrier and write something down, you panic about what to write next, and next, and next . . .

In spite of these psychological barriers, writers' minds burst with ideas, so the problem is not how to come up with ideas but how to evaluate them, sort them out, and organize them in some meaningful order into modules.

That is one of the main thrusts of this book: to show you how to create, sort out, evaluate, and organize your ideas and then to devise a comprehensive modular outline so your writing becomes a cogent, lucid, logical, and easy-to-write document.

Following is a topic outline that illustrates the logical steps this fifteen-chapter book covers.

Learning to Write the Modular Way

Organization is the most difficult—and important—aspect of writing. It is the basis of clarity. Without organization, the ideas and topics are unrelated, and readers become confused and irritated. Organization is thus a vital key to unlocking your ideas and putting them into readable writing.

Chapter 2 covers the methods of organizing material—spatial, chronological, order of increasing detail, major division order, known to known, inductive-deductive, and literary/suspense—used to make both writing and reading easier.

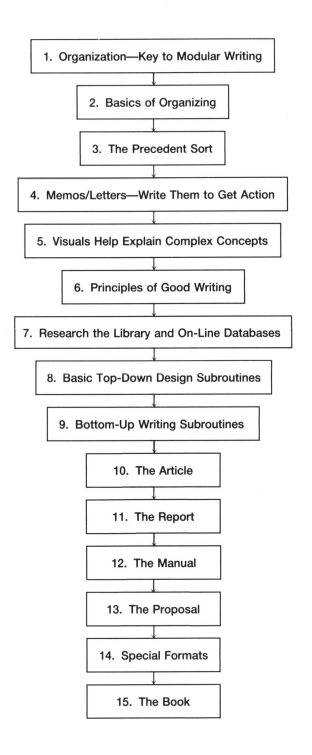

1. Organization—Key to Modular Writing

2. Basics of Organizing

3. The Precedent Sort

4. Memos/Letters—Write Them to Get Action

5. Visuals Help Explain Complex Concepts

6. Principles of Good Writing

7. Research the Library and On-Line Databases

8. Basic Top-Down Design Subroutines

9. Bottom-Up Writing Subroutines

10. The Article

11. The Report

12. The Manual

13. The Proposal

14. Special Formats

15. The Book

The Precedent Sort, my unique organizational technique, is explained in Chapter 3.

Chapter 4 eases you into composing short documents by showing you how to write short letters and memos that result in action by using the Four Part Formula: HEY! YOU! SEE? SO! HEY! and YOU! attract the reader's attention. SEE? shows the reader what you want to say. SO! draws a conclusion for the reader.

Longer documents often contain visuals (illustrations) and they must become integral parts of your design and writing. Chapter 5 shows you how to save words and clarify concepts by creating effective visuals that help to explain difficult or complex concepts.

Chapter 6 covers the principles of good writing as they specifically apply to business writing: logical word order, proper grammar, correct spelling, clear and concrete words, and effective, concise sentences.

Chapter 7 shows you how to gather and evaluate the information you'll need to write. It describes the methodology of library research so that you will locate the materials you need in the most expeditious manner, and it explains how to use the electronic libraries of the future: on-line databases.

Although special formats are required for different types of manuscripts, the basic methods of planning them are very similar. Chapter 8 covers general top-down design subroutine for researching and outlining all major types of formats.

The next step in creating a manuscript, bottom-up writing, is the subject of Chapter 9. It describes a bottom-up writing subroutine, useful for all types of formats, for converting the outline into text.

Business writing uses a number of specialized writing formats that are unique to the professions. Chapter 10 introduces the basic business document formats and details the design and writing of an article for publication. These formats—the report, the manual, the proposal, special formats (including the specification), and the book—are the subjects of Chapters 11–15.

The Appendixes contain a comprehensive listing of specialized literature resources to use for business writing and lists of on-line vendors and on-line databases.

Removing the Lead From Your Prose

Much business writing will never be read because it is nothing but leaden prose. To illustrate how turgid prose can become, even in everyday life, consider this gem:

In accordance with our previous contractual agreement, it is hereby requested that, due to circumstances beyond our control, you cease and desist in your delivery for the consecutive period after Monday, June 19, up to and including Wednesday, June 21, and that you resume, per our original agreement, on Thursday, June 22, and thereafter, until you receive further written authorization from the undersigned or its designee.

This was a note to a milkman, written by an addled business department manager. It meant:

Please skip Tuesday and Wednesday.

Which version would you prefer to write and to read? This book teaches you how to *remove the lead from your prose.*

2
Basics of Organizing

If a man can group his ideas, he is a good writer.

—Robert Louis Stevenson

In a major city, a four-story, red brick office building was scheduled to be moved to a vacant lot eleven blocks away to make room for a new freeway. Three movers were invited to present their credentials to the building's owners.

Ace Movers, the largest of the three, got the job. It immediately sent ten engineers, twenty mechanics, and four truckloads of equipment to the location. They planned to lift up the building with huge hydraulic jacks and move it on rollers to its new site. They labored long and hard, but the jacks, not sturdy enough to lift the huge building, broke each time they tried to elevate the structure. They had to abandon their hastily conceived method—and were summarily fired.

Modern Movers, the next in size, was then contracted to do the job. Modern Movers decided that thinking hard was better than brute force, so they hired eight college professors and seven computer-wise consultants who were full of ideas and good intentions. The intellectual group considered all manner of methods to move the building. They computed the elevating forces needed to lift and transport the huge structure using large blimps to hoist it up and carry it away. As their computers spewed out detailed complex calculation after calculation, the learned men and women also considered helicopters and dozens of other methods of lifting the building up all at once. But finally their calculating, thinking, and talking totally exhausted them. They theorized that it was absolutely impossible to move the building and gave up.

The building owners then moved down to Bell Movers, the tiniest of the three movers. Walter Bell, the owner, told his engineers to simplify. They weren't quite sure what he meant by that when they went with him to the building site. They walked around it and measured it carefully. After calculating, they came up with a detailed plan: Starting at the very top of the building, they would loosen and carry one brick at a time to the new location and then reassemble the building according to the detailed sketches they were going to make. It was a very simple solution. Although the actual work took many trips between locations, before long the building glistened in its new location. Bell and his employees earned special bonuses for solving the problem so effectively.

Writing an article, a report, or a book is a project much like moving the building. It's much too big a job to jump into without planning or with only good intentions. You must reduce it to a detailed and well-thought-out plan, with a series of small steps, and then accomplish each of these steps one at a time.

That is precisely what a good outline, a logical ordering of your topics and ideas, accomplishes for you. Proper organization reduces the seemingly insurmountable task of writing a huge manuscript into a series of small, easily manageable, interrelated modules, each of which can be tackled one at a time and joined together until the total manuscript is completed. Remember that all big things are made up of small things.

Steps Required to Organize

Proper organization of the material you will accumulate for your writing project requires two distinct steps: (1) categorization and (2) ordering.

Categorization consists of sorting your notes and your research material into separate categories, with the materials in each category closely related. The categories become either modules or chapters, depending on the depth and the extent to which the topics will be covered. Then you must order the chapters or modules into some logical sequence, such as chronological, spatial, major-division, or cause-to-effect. The result of these two steps (detailed in Chapters 3 and 4) is a comprehensive outline to guide your writing.

Topic Versus Sentence Outlines

Two basic types of outline forms are commonly used: topic and sentence. They can be used individually or intermixed in a single outline.

A topic outline is an abbreviated outline that lists the chapter, modules, and submodules to be covered in each specific part of a document; the book outline shown in Figure 1-1 is an example. A topic outline can be used when the specific meanings of each topic are clearly understood. For example, a topic outline for a report investigating the purchase of a number of computers for a company could list the simple headings:

- Basic computer
- Add-on equipment
- Warranty details

A sentence outline is required when a more specific definition of each topic is needed. The topics in the previous outline could be expanded into a sentence outline as follows:

- What is included in the basic equipment: turnkey operation, software, color monitors, printers?
- What add-ons are needed: extra memory, mouse and graphic table support, printer fonts?
- What does the warranty cover: in-house repair, how long before service call is responded to, weekends?

The more detailed sentence outline clarifies the topics, provides added details, and makes the writing easier and faster. Often the sentences in this type of outline can form the basis for the topic sentences for paragraphs, and they may serve as key statements for entire strings of paragraphs.

Ordering Methods

Before beginning to organize your work, select the type of ordering sequence that will best present your topics. Your material can be sequenced by either a *natural* order—the order inherent in a subject, such as a chronological or spatial order of events—or a *logical* order—one created by the writer that is based on inference or reason, such as a problem-solution order.

Outlines can be ordered in any number of possible ways. Many of these overlap, and most are reversible (past-to-future, future-to-past; near-to-far, far-to-near).

The most common ordering methods are as follows:

1. Chronological
2. Spatial
3. Sequential
4. Major division
5. Specific-to-general—general-to-specific
6. Known to unknown (analogy)
7. Importance (increasing or decreasing)
8. Cause-to-effect—effect-to-cause
9. Problem-solution
10. Comparison-contrast (advantages-disadvantages)
11. Numerical-alphabetical
12. Pro-con
13. Increasing detail
14. Literary or suspense
15. How-to-do-it

The first four methods use a natural order: the other eleven use a logical order determined by the writer.

Chronological

A chronologically ordered outline organizes the topics by the time sequence in which they occurred or should occur:

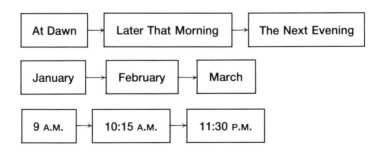

Human psychology is such that people find it much easier to understand writing that follows a familiar sequence, such as time or place. You write about the first event or the topic that occurred or should occur first, then the second in time sequence, and so on, until you reach the last event or topic. Fiction typically uses a chronological order, often interspersing flashbacks and flashforwards. In nonfiction, a chronological outline is suitable for trip reports and operating instructions.

One problem inherent in chronological order is that it intermixes both important and minor events, without proper subordination. You may be tempted to include insignificant events merely for the sake of completeness.

Spatial

The spatial order organizes topics in a geographical or physical position order:

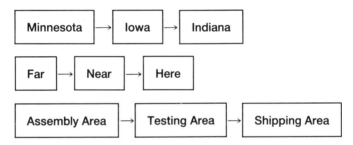

You can start at the center and move out, or go from the top to the bottom, or from left to right. The spatial order is effective when physically describing a building, a computer installation, a person, a manufacturing assembly line, or something similar.

Sequential

The sequential order organizes the steps to be performed in a sequence to assemble (or disassemble) an object or the steps required to perform a series of tests or to conduct an operation or procedure, such as:

1. Open the book.
2. Review Contents.
3. Read Chapter 1.

This order is useful for operating instructions, recipes, how-to-do-its, procedures, and tutorials.

Major Division

The major division order is used for a topic that logically divides up into natural and obvious parts. For example, a proposal or lab report is typically divided into the specific major steps performed:

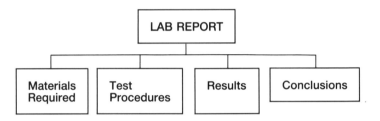

This type of format is often dictated by company or industry standards. Company organization charts also use the major division order to illustrate the functions of management hierarchy.

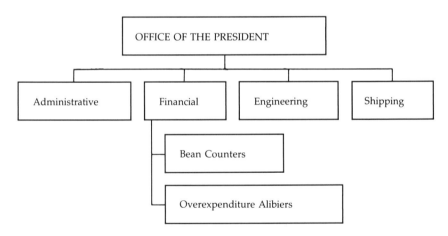

Specific to General—General to Specific

The specific-to-general and general-to-specific orders proceed from the little picture to the big picture, or vice versa, as shown in Figure 2-1.

Figure 2-1. Moving from the little picture to the big picture.

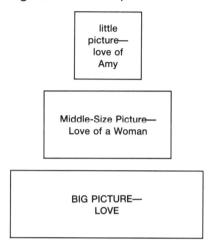

Specific to General

Also called the inductive order, the specific-to-general order starts with the facts. These facts are discussed in a logical order and used to build up to the conclusion you want to prove. For example, a promotional brochure could start by listing all the awards that company personnel have received for excellent service for one specific product. Then it could state that the same team of qualified and experienced service personnel will be servicing all of the company's new products, so customers can expect to continue to receive the same excellent service.

The specific-to-general order can also be used to catch readers' attention and to create suspense, as the following example shows:

On August 1, 1981, Paul Bell created an invention that changed the format of home computers.

The writer can then move from this specific claim to the general, explaining how and why this invention was conceived.

General to Specific

Also called the deductive order, the *general-to-specific* order starts with a general statement and then adds the facts that support the original statement. For example, a brochure on dental services might begin by stating that company's dental services are superior to all others. The balance of the brochure would cite the facts—customers' satisfaction, up-to-date automation of services, advantages offered over those of competitors—that prove the initial assertion.

Known to Unknown

The known-to-known (or analogy) order is useful for documents such as instruction manuals that explain new equipment or a new theory of operation. The writer begins with one or more facts the reader already knows and then bridges to another fact that can be deduced from the first. This bridging from one fact to another continues until the reader understands the new material. (This method is often called the professorial or teaching method.) As an example of this order, the flow of electricity in a wire is often compared to a phenomenon everyone is familiar with: the flow of pressurized water in a pipe. This type of analogy is illustrated below:

- Water pressure is equivalent to voltage.
- Rate of water flow is equivalent to current flow.
- Pipe resistance is equivalent to circuit resistance.

Importance

Items or topics can be arranged in order of increasing or decreasing importance (e.g., size, value, weight, complexity, emotional impact), depending on the desired effect.

Also called the climax order, an order of increasing importance can hold the reader's attention if the material is of sufficient interest at the beginning. For example, a doctor could discuss a series of potential treatments for a specific malady, starting out with the least effective technique and then working up to and concluding with the treatment he or she feels is best.

Conversely, an order of decreasing importance places the most important facts or data first to provide readers with a quick review of the most important points, and continuing down the importance ladder to the least important. A doctor using this technique would start out with what he or she considers the most effective treatment for a malady and then explain why he or she eliminated other possibilities. This order is also effective in providing an executive summary of the most important points at the beginning of a document and then progressing to lesser and lesser important details.

Cause to Effect–Effect to Cause

Cause-to-effect and effect-to-cause orders cover the cause(s) that resulted in a given effect(s), or vice versa.

The cause-to-effect order explains why something happened or predicts what might happen as a result of the cause, as the following examples show:

> Speeding leads to dangerous situations, which leads to an accident, which leads to injury, which leads to crippling, which leads to . . .

> Unorganized material leads to writing that is difficult to understand, which leads to reader confusion, which leads to lost sales, which leads to . . .

The effect-to-cause order, in contrast, starts with the effect (a problem or a condition) and then discusses what might have caused that effect (result)—for example:

> Accidents result from improper bicycle maintenance.

> Flooding results from heavy rain and no preventive measures.

For multiple causes and effects (either or both may be plural), an effective technique is to arrange the causes in order of increasing importance so that the first and most important cause remains dominant when the reader is later presented with the effects.

Problem-Solution

The problem-solution order is effective when it is necessary to state a problem, define and analyze what caused it, and propose a solution(s). An example of this order is a report prepared to show the causes of the collapse of a double-layer freeway and how future designs must be modified to prevent collapse.

Comparison-Contrast

Comparison-contrast compares two or more ideas or items and is sometimes linked up with the advantages or disadvantages of the items. This order is used to compare a company's products or services to those of one or more competitors—for example:

Our Product	*Competitor's Product*
More compact	Fifty percent more volume
Less costly	Costs 10 percent more
Longer lived	Longevity not guaranteed

Usually the report concludes by making one or more specific recommendations.

Numerical-Alphabetical

A numerical-alphabetical order is used when a number of arbitrary topics are to be tied together and for which no logical order or form exists. These topics can be ordered and listed using numbers or letters, along with the topic titles, to provide some semblance of organization and to refer to in the accompanying documentation:

Subjects to Be Discussed in Staff Meeting

1. Pay raises
2. Moving plant to new location
3. Company cars—personal use
4. Production problems

Pro-Con

Pro-con order conveys negative or controversial information while still maintaining a reader's goodwill:

City living	Country living
Self-teaching	Classroom teaching

For this order, both sides of a controversial question—the pro and the con—are presented. The preferred strategy is to conclude the argument with a positive statement that the reader will remember. Or you can present evidence and let the reader draw conclusions based on the evidence presented.

Increasing Detail

Newspaper stories typically use an order of increasing detail: The entire event or topic is summarized in the first paragraph, with subsequent paragraphs adding more and more detail until the writer runs out of facts or the editor runs out of patience or space and limits the column inches allocated. A news story is written that way so that it can be snipped off after any paragraph to fit the allotted space yet still contain the important facts. This type of outline is also used when presenting information to a wide variety of readers, such as when describing a new medicine to laypeople and doctors or in market research studies. Some readers will read only the summary or introductory paragraphs. Those interested in greater depth can read most or all of the document.

Literary or Suspense

The literary or suspense order reveals a little more information at a time and builds suspense up slowly to a climax at the end of the document that the writer hopes will be unexpected and entertaining. Mysteries and nonfiction humor use this order effectively.

How-to-Do-It

Finally, the how-to-do-it order of organizing, sometimes called the operational order, presents the information in the order the reader needs to follow to be able to understand and use the material. The how-to is often used in instructional material, lectures, and textbooks and is utilized in much of the material in this book and in most other how-to books.

Choosing the Most Effective Ordering Method

The ordering method you choose will be determined by the purpose of each specific topic of the document you are writing:

To Inform, to Document, or to Entertain

Chronological
Spatial
Major divisions
Increasing detail
Specific to general
Increasing or decreasing importance
How-to-do-it
Literary or suspense
Numerical-alphabetical

To Convince or to Get Action

Inductive or deductive
Pro-con
Problem-solution

To Explain or to Get Understanding

Known to unknown
Comparison-contrast
Cause to effect

Chapter 3 shows you a unique and powerful technique for organizing your material that will change your attitude about outlining forever. You can use this method for organizing a book or a chapter, an article or a technical manual, a short story or a novel. It's a technique that promises to revolutionize your writing. You'll find the Precedent Sort to be a capital idea.

3
The Precedent Sort

Prose = words in their best order.

—Samuel Coleridge

Your reader may understand the individual words in a sentence, yet still not comprehend their meaning if the ideas and concepts are not logically arranged. A method is needed to help create this logical order. The Precedent Sort, a newly developed, easy-to-use technique that simplifies arranging your topics in a logical order, fills this need.

Alphabetizing a List

To see how the P-Sort functions, consider this list of randomly organized words that need to be alphabetized:

    manuscript
    computer
    pen
    book
    paper

These words will be alphabetized by comparing two adjacent words at a time. If the second word belongs ahead of the first word alphabetically, the order of the two words will be interchanged; otherwise their order will remain unchanged. These comparisons by pairs will be continued until all possible comparisons have been made. To organize n

words (or *n* cards), *n* minus 1 comparison rounds are needed. Each subsequent round requires one less comparison, until the final round, where only one comparison is needed. For the example here, five words are going to be alphabetized, so $n = 5$. This requires *n* minus 1 $(5-1)$ or four rounds of comparison by pairs.

Prepare for the P-Sort by writing each word on a separate 3- by 5-inch card, then stack the cards in the order shown in Figure 3-1. (Index cards are ideal for manipulating when performing the P-Sort because they are easier to handle and more durable than paper.) This first round has four steps.

Round 1

1. Compare the card with the word *manuscript* on it with the card with the word *computer* on it. Since *computer* belongs alphabetically before *manuscript*, interchange the order of the first two cards. The new order after the first comparison by pairs is:

   computer
   manuscript
   pen
   book
   paper

2. Compare the second or *manuscript* card with the *pen* card. Since *manuscript* belongs earlier alphabetically, the order of these two cards remains unchanged.
3. Compare the third card, *pen*, with the fourth card, *book*. *Book* belongs earlier alphabetically, so interchange the order of these two cards and arrive at this result:

   computer
   book
   manuscript
   paper
   pen

4. Compare *pen* with *paper*. *Paper* belongs earlier alphabetically, so interchange the order of these last two cards. The result of this final comparison of the first round is illustrated in Figure 3-2.

By the end of this first round of comparisons by pairs, we have performed what is called in computer programming a "bubble sort."

The words that belong earlier alphabetically are slowly bubbling up to the top of the pile. The sort can also be called a "sinking sort," since words belonging later alphabetically are sinking to the bottom of the pile. By the end of this first round, *pen* has sunk to the bottom to become the last card alphabetically. You are now ready for Round 2.

Round 2

1. Compare the first two cards in Figure 3-2: *computer* and *manuscript*. *Computer* belongs earlier alphabetically, so do not interchange their order. The order remains as shown in the figure.
2. Compare the second card, *manuscript*, with the third card, *book*. *Book* belongs earlier alphabetically and is moved ahead of *manuscript*. The new order is as follows:

   computer
   book
   manuscript
   paper
   pen

3. Compare *manuscript* with *paper*. *Manuscript* belongs earlier alphabetically so remains in place. The third step completes the second round of comparisons by pairs, since *pen* has already been properly placed in the last position of the order. The order at the end of the Round 2 is as shown in Figure 3-3.

Round 3

1. Compare *computer* with *book* (Figure 3-3). Since *book* belongs earlier alphabetically, interchange these first two cards. You now have:

   book
   computer
   manuscript
   paper
   pen

2. Compare *computer* with *manuscript*. *Computer* belongs earlier alphabetically so remains in the same place.

The second step completes Round 3 (Figure 3-4) since the last two cards have already been placed in order by the first two rounds.

Figure 3-1.   Initial order of cards for alphabetizing.

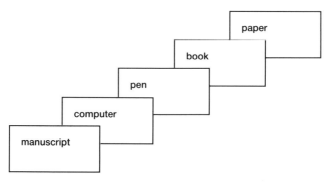

The cards can be held in a one-on-top-of-the-other stack for easier manipulation. They are shown split apart in these figures simply for illustration purposes.

Figure 3-2.   Order of cards for alphabetizing at end of Round 1.

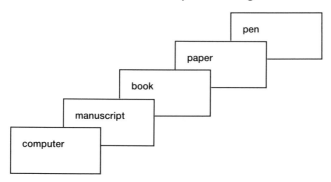

Figure 3-3.   Order of cards for alphabetizing at end of Round 2.

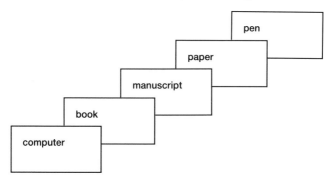

Figure 3-4. Order of cards for alphabetizing at end of Round 3.

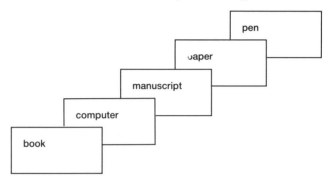

For the fourth and final round remember that five cards are used, so *n* minus 1 or 5 minus 1 means four rounds are needed to complete the organizing:

Round 4

1. Compare *book* with *computer* (Figure 3-4). Since *book* belongs earlier alphabetically, it remains in the same place.

The cards have now been completely organized in increasing alphabetical order. The final order is as shown in Figure 3-4.

This may have seemed to be a laborious process just to organize five words in alphabetical order. The example was purposely made simple so the basic idea could be imparted easily without becoming tangled in the details of determining precedence. The next example of Precedent Sort will show how to organize topics in a document. The illustration will use only five topics, but remember that the basic procedures can easily be extended to organize up to thirty to fifty or more topics before it becomes unwieldy.

Organizing Topics

For this example, assume you have been assigned the topic of preparing an operating manual for your company's video cassette recorder. In the exercise, you will organize the five chapters you have been asked to write. Later, you could organize the modules within each chapter using the identical procedure.

The five chapters have been assigned the following titles listed in random order:

preventive maintenance
installation
operation
troubleshooting
summary of features

Begin by writing each chapter title on a separate 3- by 5-inch card, and stack the cards in the order shown in Figure 3-5. Again, they may be manipulated in a one-on-top-of-the-other order for convenience in handling.

Round 1

1. Compare the first and second cards to determine which topic logically should be discussed earlier in the operating manual. Logically, installation comes before preventive maintenance (the VCR had better be working long before it requires maintenance), so interchange the order of the first two cards to arrive at this order:

   installation
   preventive maintenance
   operation
   troubleshooting
   summary of features

2. Compare the second card, preventive maintenance, with the third card, operation. Because the user must know how to operate the VCR before any maintenance is required, these two cards must be interchanged.

   installation
   operation
   preventive maintenance
   troubleshooting
   summary of features

3. Compare the third card, preventive maintenance, with the fourth card, troubleshooting. Certainly preventive maintenance should be covered earlier because the purpose of preventive mainte-

nance is either to make troubleshooting unnecessary or to post-pone it as long as possible, so do not interchange the order of these two cards. The order remains unchanged from Step 2.

4. Compare the fourth card, troubleshooting, with the fifth, summary of features. Certainly the latter topic should be covered before troubleshooting, so interchange the order of these last two cards.

At the end of the first round of comparisons, the cards should be ordered as shown in Figure 3-6.

Round 2

1. Compare the installation card with operation (Figure 3-6). Logically the VCR must be installed before it can be operated, so the order of cards remains unchanged.

2. Compare the operation and preventive maintenance cards. Because VCR operation must be covered before preventive maintenance is required, the order again remains unchanged.

3. Compare the preventive maintenance and summary of features cards. The summary of features must be covered earlier since it will be the first section the users will read: in other words, the summary will serve as an introduction to the VCR and its features. Interchange the order of these two cards.

The order at the conclusion of the second round of comparisons is shown in Figure 3-7.

Round 3

1. Compare the installation and operation cards (Figure 3-7). Clearly they are already in the correct order.

2. Compare the second and third cards: operation and summary of features. The latter topic is sequentially earlier, so interchange the order of these two cards.

The results at the end of Round 3 are shown in Figure 3-8.

Round 4

1. Compare the first two cards in Figure 3-8. Summary of features is the logical choice for the first and introductory chapter in the manual, so interchange the order of the summary of features and installation.

Figure 3-5. Initial order of cards for topic organization.

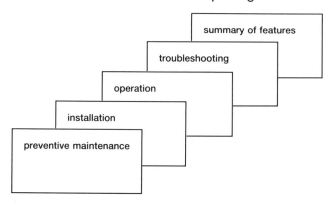

Figure 3-6. Order of cards for topic organization at end of Round 1.

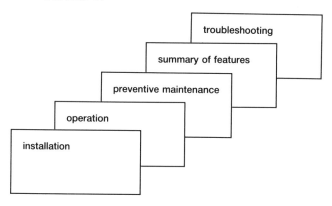

Figure 3-7. Order of cards for topic organization at end of Round 2.

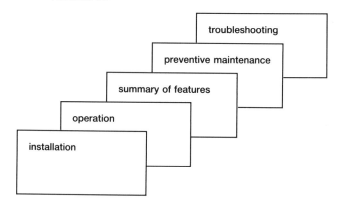

Figure 3-8. Order of cards for topic organization at end of Round 3.

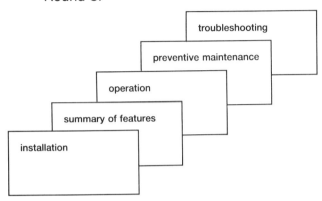

Figure 3-9. Final order of topics.

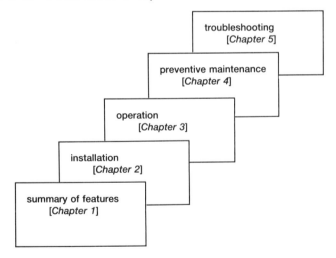

The final order of topics accomplished by use of the Precedent Sort is shown in Figure 3-9. The summary of features module has bubbled to the top to become Chapter 1.

Although the Precedent Sort is a "formula," you still must make subjective judgments for all the pairings. Your judgment of which topic should be covered earlier may differ from the author's, but that's where your creativity comes in. The process does indeed have room for individual creativity. That's precisely what makes it so universal in its applications.

The basic principle of the Precedent Sort is to compare only two topics at one time and then decide which topic should be discussed earlier in the document. Instead of a confusing, complex problem of simultaneously trying to compare, shuffle, manipulate, and organize twenty to fifty or more different topics, organizing becomes a simple task of repeatedly comparing and subjectively ordering only two topics at one time.

Guidelines for Using Precedent Sort

With Precedent Sort, you can take any number of topics (up to about fifty before the procedure becomes unwieldy and time-consuming), written in any form (phrases, sentences, questions), and organize them in a sequential pattern that makes your writing flow logically and easily from one topic to the next. It's much easier to don a pair of blinders, focus your mind, and concentrate fully on only two topics at a time, side by side, and decide which belongs earlier than to confuse the issue by trying to compare and juggle fifty or more topics at the same time.

Observe these three important guidelines when using the Precedent Sort:

1. Proceed logically from the first card to the last in sequential order. Don't jump around, or your results will not be accurate, the comparisons by pairs will be confusing, and the decisions more difficult to make.

2. Before making your comparisons by pairs, be sure you under-stand precisely what each topic is and means. If you are uncertain, write out a statement, summary, or paragraph on the card to define precisely what each topic means before you start to compare. Write as much as you need to define each topic precisely for yourself.

3. Don't decide the order of the topics is unimportant and neglect to interchange the order of the cards. Judge each comparison, weighing all of the factors as best you can. If the proper order isn't clear-cut, just guess. You must make a decision or the process won't work. If subjects are that close, the order probably doesn't matter. And if you're

dissatisfied with the final results, you can always iterate and change them around later.

A Caution

Don't be misled into thinking that the Precedent Sort is a mechanical, robotlike way of organizing topics. It's not. You still must use your judgment and creativity, just as you do when you use all writing formulas. The P-Sort simply provides the mechanics; it is a procedure to help you break down a huge, perplexing problem into a series of one-on-one, orderly, logical, individual decisions.

The outline you initially create need not be static. If there are compelling reasons to change the order around later, do so. If there are topics to be added or deleted, do so. It's a hundred times easier to work with an outline that is neatly organized than to try to organize fifty or more randomly listed topics.

Other Applications for P-Sort

The P-Sort has many other applications, including the following:

- Scheduling tasks and itemizing the order in which jobs must be accomplished to reach a goal in a logical, efficient manner.
- Ranking the topics in a sales brochure or report, listing the most important features first.
- Arranging a large group of items in a numerical, alphabetical, or chronological order.
- Assigning jobs. Use two Precedent Sorts. With one sort, rank employees in order of their competence. Then use a second sort to rank the jobs that need to be done in their order of difficulty. Assign the best employee to the most difficult job, second best to the second most difficult job, and so on down the line.
- Organizing tasks that you need to do every day in a required time or spatial sequence, by difficulty of task, or some other order.
- Arranging ideas that must be sold or justified in order of difficulty, such as in a technical proposal where you should spend the most time discussing the most difficult problems to be solved.
- Arranging a big decision into a series of lesser decisions that must be settled first (for example, when buying a computer).

- Judging contests ranging from speeches (ranking the speakers for first, second, and third prizes), to cattle shows, to cake-baking competitions, to beauty contests.

In the next chapter, you're going to learn how to write and respond to letters and memos, the most common and most useful documents you will encounter in your profession.

4

Memos and Letters: How to Write Them to Get Action

Lean writing thrusts the essential ideas vigorously forward, so learn to trim the fat from your memos and letters.

—Anonymous

In a survey conducted by the Accountemps Personnel Agency, 200 corporate executives were questioned on how they spent their time. The executives said they wasted 32 minutes a day—128 hours a year—reading and writing unnecessary memos. One of the major goals of this chapter is to help you eliminate those wasted 32 minutes a day so you can use that time more effectively.

Another goal is to show you how to shorten your communications without losing effectiveness. A U.S. Department of Agriculture study found that an estimated 85 percent of the work force of the average American industry is involved in various forms of paper handling and more than 15 percent of all business letters are written to clarify earlier written letters.

We do live in a paper world; it is a woefully inefficient one, and has been as long as paper has existed. Even Shakespeare recognized the problem when he said, "The letter is too long by half a mile."

Before covering the longer writing formats—the article, manual, proposal, and report—we'll examine the simplest of all business communications: the common, yet important and useful, memo and letter. Memos and letters are actually mini-reports, so many of the principles you'll learn in this chapter can be directly applied to the longer-format documents discussed in later chapters.

In memos and letters, as well as in longer documents, brevity is a virtue. Many readability studies have confirmed that long sentences are more difficult to understand and require more effort to read than short sentences. "Get out!" is obviously briefer and much more effective than "Remove yourself from this place immediately!"

Memos and letters provide excellent opportunities to practice and develop brevity and conciseness. Your primary goal in writing these communications is to make them easy to read and easy to understand. If you are successful, readers will be receptive to what you're writing rather than irritated by a poorly written, confusing communication.

Getting to the Point: Overcoming the Most Common Fault of Memos

Everyone who must write as part of his or her job—and that includes virtually everyone in the business world—is required to compose memos and letters to document certain facts or to request or communicate information, either from within one's company or from an outside individual or company. The letter or memo is an extremely important form of communication. Learn it well, and the longer documents will be easier to write.

The most common, glaring fault of memos and letters is circumlocution. It can be cured by this simple advice:

> **Get to the point!**

In delivering a speech, the first minute is crucial because during this short period, everyone in the audience is listening. If the first minute doesn't capture the audience, the speech will fail.

The same situation exists in writing. Since most people read the first paragraph or so of a document, the first few sentences are crucial; they must hook the reader into reading on. If you lose your reader after the first few sentences, your memo or letter will likely go unread.

If you get to the point right away and grab your reader's interest, the document has a much better chance of being read and acted upon.

People who are reading a letter or memo want to find out right away what it's all about. They don't have the patience to wade through a long and possibly overdrawn history of the problem. The detailed background of the situation can come later if it's needed at all. Get to the point as quickly as you can.

- The Lord's Prayer contains 68 words.
- The Gettysburg Address contains 266 words.
- The Ten Commandments contain 297 words.
- The Declaration of Independence contains 300 words.
- A U.S. government publication setting the price of cabbage contains an incredible 29,111 words!
- Truly the shortest and most moving sentence in the New Testament is "Jesus wept."

Getting to the point:

- Forces you to think succinctly and to compose a short memo or letter.
- Gives the reader enough information to decide if he or she should continue reading.
- Results in a document that is likely to be read.
- Saves time and money for both writer and reader.
- Makes the letter or memo easier to write and to read.

The Four Part Formula

Many people do not invest the time required to plan a memo or letter. Instead, they start writing right away, putting down whatever comes into their head in whatever scrambled order it occurs. The unfortunate result is a long, meandering letter that takes forever to get to the point.

To help you organize your thoughts for all kinds of writing, the Four Part Formula—HEY! YOU! SEE? SO!—is ideal.* It makes letter and memo writing easy, efficient, complete, and almost formulalike in its precision. It is based on the fundamental way that people react:

*Described in Walter S. Campbell, *Writing Non-Fiction* (Boston: The Writer, 1961).

1. HEY! The first part of the formula requires that you hook the reader's attention with some interesting phrase or an attention-getting statement, such as:

Baseball is America's *second favorite sport.*
Baseball is also America's *favorite sport.*

2. YOU! Remember that most letters and memos are uninvited, so you have to give the recipient a good reason to read it. To do this, bring the reader into the topic right away. Convince the reader, your one-on-one audience, that what you said in your opening, and what you are going to say in the rest of your memo or report, is important and interesting. Your reader is primarily interested in himself or herself, not in you or the company you're writing for. To bring the YOU into your document, use something like this:

Do you realize that if it weren't for baseball, you wouldn't be able to enjoy Cracker Jacks?

3. SEE? This is the main part, the body, of your written communication. In this section you present your facts, your story. Show the reader how you prove your thesis; demonstrate the points you want to make; deliver the message you have to give, such as:

At a baseball game, hot dogs taste like filet mignon, the popcorn is crunchier . . .

4. SO! Convince the reader in this final part that he or she has profited by reading your communication. Leave behind some closing thought, idea, or conclusion or a call to some kind of action:

So, go out to the ball game and cheer loudly for your favorites. Baseball is one of the world's best tranquilizers.

Whether you realize it or not, you use the Four Part Formula many times a day. For example, suppose you see your co-worker, Floyd, walking down the hall at work.

"Floyd!" you call out. (HEY!)

Turning, Floyd walks over to you. "Yes?" he asks, frowning, tugging at his ear.

"How'd you like to go to the ball game tonight?" (YOU!)

"Who's playing?" Floyd responds, pursing his lips.

"The Dodgers. Got an extra ticket. Ashburn is pitching, and Schaffitz is catching. Should be a super game!" (SEE?)

"Sound great," Floyd smiles. "Okay."

"Pick you up at seven," you say. (SO!)

There! You've used the Four Part Formula without even thinking about it. It's a potent natural formula, based on the way all people normally react.

In advertising, the Four Part Formula is used extensively:

Our Hartford tires are triple-steel-belted [HEY!] to keep you [YOU!] safe on the roads. Tested on rough, washboard roads and high-speed freeways, Hartford tires show no wear after 5 million miles. [SEE?] They're on sale now, at your local dealer. Buy a set today! [SO!]

Even a simple memo should use this formula:

TO: Adeline Hansen
FROM: Thomas Welch
SUBJECT: Lab Tests on Solvent X-23 [HEY!]

The lab tests you [YOU!] performed last Friday were not documented properly. We need your complete report so we can distribute copies to Research. [SEE?]
Please complete the report by this Friday, January 13, or you'll be pulled off the project. [SO!]

When you start using the HEY! YOU! SEE? SO! formula consciously, you'll find that your writing has become more interesting, effective, and concise and much easier, almost formulalike, to write.

Good organization and the proper way of presenting your information are at least two-thirds of the battle of business writing.

The Body of a Letter or Memo

The body is truly the meat of letter and memo formats. But before you write the body, you must do three things: (1) Jot down what you want to say; (2) organize your thoughts; and (3) apply the Four Part Formula.

Jot Down What You Want to Say

Jot down what you want to say in whatever random order your thoughts occur to you and in any format—questions, statements, key words, or something else. Don't worry about organization or grammar at this point.

Suppose your supervisor (a terrible writer) has asked you to write a letter to the author of an article describing a new database software program requesting more information about the product. You make the following random notes as a result of your conversation with your supervisor:*

How much memory is required? (SEE?)
Which IBM PC versions is the program compatible with?
(SEE?)
Availability? Delivery? Cost? (SEE?)
Request spec sheets. (SO!)
Can it be used in a network? (SEE?)
Can it be adapted for mailing lists? (SEE?)

Apply the Four Part Formula

When you apply the Four Part Formula, remember to keep foremost in your mind the first and most fundamental rule in letter and memo writing: Get to the point!

Generate the HEY! and get to the point at the same time, preferably in the first sentence or two. This is easy when the first paragraph in a letter or memo is one or two sentences that summarize the letter. In starting, bring the *you*, the addressee, into the letter before you bring in the *I* or *we*. And don't overuse the *I* or *we*. Try this for a draft of the first paragraph:

> Your article [YOU!] in *PC Data News* on your new database software program was interesting [HEY!]. We need more information about it so we can evaluate its applicability to our databases.

Next, cover the questions listed (SEE?), grouping them logically. (If you have many questions or statements to organize, order them with the Precedent Sort.)

*A tentative assignment of topics to be covered in the SEE and SO sections can be made at this point. If required, they can be rearranged when the letter is written.

Our company is considering using your database software for a new customer database. However, we need more data before committing our entire company to your program. Specifically, our questions are:

1. Can your database be adapted for mailing lists?
2. Is your program now on the market? If so:
   a. Please quote price and delivery for a single PC installation and for a network version.
   b. Do you have a demo program available for evaluation?
   c. How large a database can you accommodate?
3. Is a Macintosh version available?
4. How much RAM is required?
5. Which IBM PC versions is it compatible with?

Note that all questions pertaining to price and delivery have been grouped together, and they are short, specific, and direct. When you number and list items, as I did in the example, you're likely to create short, concise statements. As you review your draft, you will probably come up with a few more relevant questions to ask. Often when you're writing or reviewing a document, one thought will trigger another, which will trigger another, and another. And that leads to another caution: Don't be *too* comprehensive.

Memos and letters of over a page are likely to discourage the recipient from reading your communication. If your document is more than one page long, see if you can eliminate some fluff or redundancy. Limiting your communication to one page forces you to get to the point in a few words. The discipline of concise writing is an important adjunct to clear thinking.

Finally, arrange the remainder of the questions in the so! the request for action:

We need a prompt reply since we must solidify our network software requirements for our Preliminary Design Review meeting next month. If your program meets our requirements, it will be used in all our networks nationwide. Also please send spec sheets on your database program so we can verify its capacity and operating parameters. [so!]

The last paragraph wraps it all up, holds up a carrot (the possibility of the program's being used in their nationwide networks), tells the addressee why you're interested in the software program, and requests data sheets. The final paragraph shouldn't be more than one or two sentences.

One of the biggest problems with conclusions is that the recipient doesn't understand specifically what action is required. So when you write a conclusion, make sure the action you seek is defined and made clear to your reader.

General Cosmetics/Guidelines

For every letter and memo, observe certain guidelines:

1. *Paragraph often.* A one-paragraph letter, particularly if it's very long, looks formidable. A reader is reluctant to tackle such a complex-looking document.

2. *Keep your sentences short,* fewer than about seventeen words on the average. By the time your reader gets to the end of a long sentence, he or she forgets what it's all about.

3. *Provide adequate margins* at the top, bottom and sides (1 to 1½ inches). A crowded letter results from poor planning and biases your reader against its contents even before starting to read.

4. *Don't be afraid to use contractions.* They are not only acceptable in today's business world, they are desirable. Contractions make a letter or memo sound less formal. "I'm enclosing . . ." sounds a lot friendlier than the trite "Enclosed please find . . ."

5. *Use bullets, lists, and numbered items* to break up the monotony of solid text—but use them judiciously.

6. *If the letter is fewer than about ten lines long, double space the final typed copy* and leave a large margin at the top so the top of the page won't seem crowded.

7. *Keep a photocopy of everything you write,* no matter how trivial. You never know when you'll need to refer to it.

8. *Maintain a "you" attitude.* Don't write "*We* are happy to inform you . . ." but "*You* will be happy to know . . ." When you compose a letter or memo, you're writing to some person(s). Keep this individual(s) in mind when you write—the *you* who will be reading it. The same advice holds for you, the writer. Use "I" instead of "the writer" or "the undersigned." Samuel Coleridge wrote, "What comes from the heart, goes to the heart." It's still good advice for any kind of writing.

9. *Courtesy has not gone out of style.* Ralph Waldo Emerson's words still apply today: "Life is not so short but there is always enough time for courtesy."

Memos vs. Letters: A Definition

Up to this point I've treated memos and letters as the same, but there are differences. Since the memo is somewhat simpler, we'll cover that first.

Memos

A memo is a written communication within a company; therefore, it has no salutation (Greetings Herkimer) or complimentary close (Cordially). Typically a memo has five essential parts:

1. Date
2. Whom it's addressed to
3. Whom it's from
4. The subject
5. The body

When you write a memo, your primary aim should be to communicate information concisely and clearly. The effort required to write, read, and understand a memo should be minimal.

One of the biggest problems facing inexperienced writers is the fear of the blank page. Their mind becomes a blank, their fingers become paralyzed, and any words they force on the paper are trite, awkward, and inappropriate.

But there is a solution to this dilemma. Most people probably do not feel as if they're facing a blank page when given a form to fill out (unless it's an income tax form). A form asks specific questions to answer in any random order you choose. It even has space tentatively allocated for each answer. The forms provided in Figures 4-1 and 4-2 are designed to help overcome the fear of the blank page. You can have these forms typed up and store them in your word processor, or you can photocopy them and use them to draft memos. When your final draft is typed or retyped, the prompting statements can be deleted. The result is an easily written memo that gets to the point and is concise, readable, and effective.

Using a standard form for writing memos and letters has several advantages:

- They save time for both writer and reader.
- Because standard information is included and located in fixed places and in a definite order on the form, memos and letters are easier to read, and it is easier to locate certain information.

Figure 4-1. Form for memo notes.

Items to Be Covered in Memo	Order

A. _____

_____   _____

B. _____

_____   _____

C. _____

_____   _____

D. _____

_____   _____

E. _____

_____   _____

F. _____

_____   _____

G. _____

_____   _____

H. _____

_____   _____

Action Required: _____

_____

_____

- The headings jog the writer's memory to ensure that all the information is included in the proper order.

To use the form in Figure 4-1, first list the items you want to cover in your memo in whatever order they occur to you. Then indicate in the "Order" column which item should be covered first, second, third

Figure 4-2. Memo format.

Date: _____

To: _____

From: _____

Info Copies to: _____

_____

Subject: _____

_____

Reference(s): _____

_____

Summary Paragraph (HEY! YOU!): _____

_____

_____

_____

Body (SEE?): _____

_____

_____

_____

_____

Action (SO!): _____

_____

_____

and so on. If you have a lot of items, use the Precedent Sort to order them. Finally, identify the action desired.

Now you're ready to tackle the memo itself using the form in Figure 4-2.

▪ *Date.* The date provides important information. It tells how old the memo is and when an answer is due, and it supplies a date for a chronological file and to refer to when replying.

▪ *To.* List the person(s) to whom the memo is addressed for action.

▪ *Info Copies To.* If you send info copies to certain key individuals, you'll stand a much better chance of the recipient's paying attention to your requests, particularly if he or she knows that supervisors are also receiving copies of the same memo. But you can overdo it. Don't send Info copies to all manner of people on trivial items. They'll soon mark you down as a chronic complainer and ignore you. Judiciously used, however, this distribution technique will help you quickly obtain the results you want.

▪ *Subject and Reference.* The subject gives your reader a quick idea of the purpose of the memo, so be specific. For example, don't use "Progress Report"; instead, use "Progress Report—Vineland Project, Period Ending 31 July."

The reference can be to a specific earlier memo, a contract number, a program, or something else. The reference is useful when replying to or filing the memo or when digging up reference information. Again, be specific (e.g., "Contract 243F90-6E, Section 115, Paragraph 4b"). A reference is not necessary for all communications.

▪ *Summary.* A vital part of writing, the one-sentence summary disciplines you to get to the point. "Program King Cotton is now two weeks behind schedule and will continue to slip schedule unless two more cotton-picking machines are immediately allocated to the project" certainly gets to the point.

▪ *Body.* To generate the body, take the items from your memo notes form (Figure 4-1), and write them out in narrative sentences in the order you noted at the right of the items. Apply the memo and letter guidelines discussed earlier as you write. You'll find that this technique is a simple, orderly, and effective way to write memos. It's almost as easy as substituting numbers in a formula, turning the crank, and coming up with the answer: a finished memo.

▪ *Action.* The action paragraph is what your memo was written for. Everything you have said so far leads up to this short, hard-hitting paragraph. Take the notes from the memo notes form (Figure 4-1), and convert them to one or, at most, two sentences on the memo format form (Figure 4-2). Don't leave this paragraph open-ended. Request a specific action by a specific date. This will also serve to remind you to follow up and see that the required action has been accomplished.

Letters

A letter is a written communication to someone outside your company. It isn't much different from a memo except that it is friendlier and includes a salutation and closing. The same ideas discussed for memos also apply to letters, and you can use the forms supplied in Figures 4-1 and 4-2. About the only difference in the two forms is the physical layout.

A wide variety of physical layouts is possible for letters, including a balanced block, semiblock, and full-block styles, plus open or closed punctuation. I prefer the semiblock style of letter, with open punctuation (Figure 4-3). Paragraphs are indented so you know where a new subject begins, unlike that of the block style. The address and salutation are on the left, the closing on the right.

- *Salutations.* The salutation in a letter is a greeting, much like the conversational "Good morning" or "Hi." I've never understood why we still use such archaic and inappropriate greetings as "Dear Sir" or "My dear Madam." Nobody uses such stuffy phrases in conversation, and neither should they in letters. I much prefer to use such salutations as "Hi George" to someone I know well, or "Good Morning, Mrs. Calabash" or "Greetings, Mr. Smith" to someone I haven't met. When I'm writing to an organization and don't have a name to address, I use "Good morning," or "Hello," plain and simple.

- *Complimentary Close.* The same advice on stuffiness holds true for the complimentary close of a letter. Why the archaic "Yours truly" has been used for a couple of hundred years puzzles me. We never say goodbye that way, so why should we use it in a letter? It's much simpler to close with "Cordially," "Sincerely," or "Thanks," depending on your audience.

When you have to reply to a specific letter, follow these guidelines:

1. Read through the letter, underlining important points.
2. Note in the margin your responses to the questions.
3. Attach the letter to your reply so your secretary (or you) can obtain the proper address and computer or file references where required.
4. Refer to the letter you're answering right away so the reader will know what's coming.

Figure 4-3.   Semiblock style for a letter.

April 1, 1995

Professor Henry Aldrich
Grimm State Hospital
Tallahassee, R.I. 10293
Subject: Psycho-Ceramic article in <u>Normal Psychology</u>,
          February 1991.

Greetings, Professor Aldrich,

Your recent article in <u>Normal Psychology</u> fascinated
me. My boss is definitely the psycho-ceramic (crack-pot)
type that you so skillfully described. It seems as though
your article was written specifically about him. [HEY! YOU!]
My boss has fallen head-over-heels in love with our new
computer and prefers it to human companionship. He has
automated everything in our company and is laying every-
body off, two people (a binary number, of course) at a time.
[SEE?]
But I'm an expert programmer and I can plant a virus in
his program so contagious that he'll completely lose faith
in the binary beast. Do you think he'll crack up completely if the computer crashes and fails him? [SEE?]
Please advise me before Friday the thirteenth since
that's my last day at World Wide. [SO!]

Thanks,

Phigg Newton

Phigg Newton
Number 10 Downing
Elstonville, Tex. 99999

Using Humor

Most business writing is so dull that you start yawning after reading the title, and by the end of the first paragraph, you're sound asleep. It doesn't have to be this way. Business writing can be lively and interesting without detracting from that most important requirement of all business writing: Make it easy for the reader to understand. Judicious use of humor reinforces and makes more enjoyable reading about things complex. "A soft answer turneth away wrath," the Bible tells us. I'll paraphrase that: "A humorous letter bringeth delight to the reader."

5
Using Visuals to Explain Complex Concepts

A picture shows me at a glance what it takes dozens of pages of a book to expound.

—Ivan Turgenev

Most complex concepts cannot be explained by words alone. Visuals— line drawings, photographs, charts, tables, graphs—are needed, along with text, to describe how such concepts function. Visuals also break up the formidable appearance of a solid page of text. Effective use of visuals not only makes writing easier, it results in a document that is much easier to understand.

Tentatively plan which visuals you're going to use before you write the text so that the visuals form an integral part of your document rather than seeming to be tacked on at the end as afterthoughts. Visuals and text must work in concert, synergistically, each dependent on the other, to describe an object, a process, an idea, a concept.

The text should abstract from the visual enough information to help readers understand the significance of the illustration. Do not, however, repeat in the text the information contained in the visual. The text is supposed to amplify and complement the visual information. To make sure that text and visuals work together, follow these proven guidelines:

- *Use the precise, identical names in the text that you use in the visuals.* This is one of the single most confusing deficiencies in business writing. When you call something a "component" in the visual and refer to it as a "subassembly" in the text, you're injecting unnecessary confusion. It's difficult enough trying to grasp complex principles without having to struggle to interpret names that are slightly different.

- *Use many visuals.* They save considerable text and make most material easier to understand.

- *Keep sentences and paragraphs short.* White space gives your readers' eyes and minds a much-needed rest. A full-page paragraph presents a frightening clump of information to be confronted with. Your average sentence length should be about sixteen to eighteen words at the most; longer sentences make for difficult reading. Do mix some long sentences with short ones, however, to break up the monotony and to avoid singsong reading.

- *Repeat facts; summarize often.* Lengthy descriptions are often difficult to understand. Summaries help prepare the reader for what you are about to say and for reviewing what you just said to make sure it's clear. It's much better to have some redundancy and some repetition than to risk befuddling your reader. Your reader can choose to skip over redundancy, after all.

- *Define abbreviations the first time they're used*—for example, "The RAM (random access memory) provides storage for lost bits."

You can modify, add to, or delete visuals during the designing and writing processes. Here, too, it's much easier to make changes when you have a plan to modify than no plan at all.

Word-Orientation Versus Visual-Orientation

Visuals, a term that encompasses such items as line drawings, graphs, curves, photographs, pie charts, and tables, have been a vital part of writing as long as books have existed. The earliest example of a visual used to supplement text was found in an Egyptian papyrus from about 1980 B.C. So visuals have been with us for centuries.

Most writers are word oriented; they try to explain everything using only words. Certainly in the past, the pre–personal computer age, visuals were difficult for word-oriented people, few of them artists, to create. But more and more easy-to-use computer graphic programs are becoming available and function with most word processing programs.

This combination of word power and easy-to-use graphic power will help convert many prose persons into picture-prose persons as they learn how to use visuals effectively to supplement and strengthen textual material.

Using a PC, writers can experiment with different types of presentations, different orientations, and different scales to obtain the best product. Visuals can be evaluated and edited on the screen; material can be added, deleted, or moved. Visuals can be expanded or made smaller, curves and bars can be filled in with patterns. Because of the lightning speed of the PC, these changes can be input and their results viewed almost instantaneously.

Basic Visuals

This chapter discusses the basic types of visuals that can be used and the functions, applications, and advantages of each. The visuals covered are illustrated in the following figure:

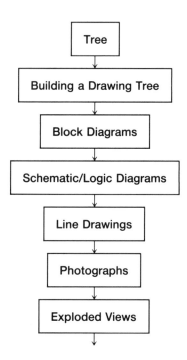

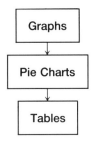

The Tree

So designated because it resembles a tree with branches, the versatile tree is one of the most common, versatile, and easy-to-construct visuals. It displays the top-to-bottom makeup of the subject (an organization, a process, a procedure, or an object) and diagrams the many small items that add up to form the largest or top assembly item. The tree illustrates how the items relate to each other in relative size and importance. The organization chart in Figure 5-1 depicting the hierarchy of a company is an example of a tree.

Figure 5-1. Tree depicting a company hierarchy.

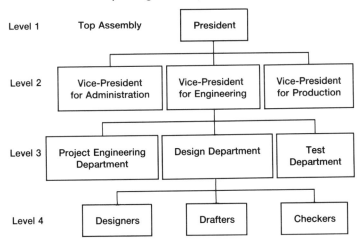

Fundamentals of Trees

Here are some fundamental characteristics of properly constructed trees:

- Elements of equal importance (e.g., size or complexity) are drawn on the same physical level (for example, all vice-presidents in Figure 5-1 are on Level 2).
- Each block contains a brief self-explanatory title that describes the component or the function the block represents.
- The tree may be expanded to as many levels as required. For complex equipment, such as an aircraft, twenty to thirty or more drawing levels may exist, from the top assembly drawing of the complete aircraft down to the brackets and metal assemblies of the smallest components.
- Illustrated on a single sheet, the tree provides a quick, graphic picture of the basic elements making up the top assembly—how they relate to each other and their relative level of importance. When used for a product to be manufactured, the tree lists all the drawings that must be created before production can begin.
- The tree shows top-down organization but not necessarily the sequence or left-to-right assembly order. (Creating that assembly order will be illustrated in the next module of this chapter.)
- As you move down the tree, the components become smaller and smaller, less and less complex, and generally more numerous.

Building a Tree

The procedure for building a tree will be illustrated by a simple example. Assume you want to diagram the basic components that make up a house and the basic sequence of steps required to build it.

First you must visualize the end result (the completed house). Then you design it from the top down, moving to smaller and smaller components until the level is reached at which you can begin the initial construction. A house should first be visualized as completely assembled and surrounded by plantings, fences, and sidewalks. Once the overall concept is decided on, the house must be broken down successively into smaller and smaller parts, until you reach the nails, the boards, and the concrete—the items that can be worked, shaped, formed, and joined.

For example: To illustrate the process of using a tree, a simple house is comprised of roof, walls, framing, foundation, and floors. Add these to the diagram of a house to get a simple house tree (or is it a tree house?) like this:

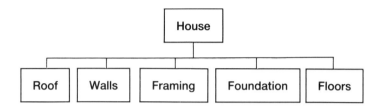

The diagram shows the basic components comprising a simple house but not the logical order in which these components should be constructed to build a house. To do this, apply the Precedent Sort:

1. Write the name of each component on individual 3- by 5-inch cards (Figure 5-2).
2. Compare the Roof and Walls cards. Certainly the roof should go up as soon as possible to provide shelter for the workers adding the walls and to protect the floors, so interchange the order to:
   Walls
   Roof
   Framing
   Foundation
   Floors

Figure 5-2.   Initial order of cards for constructing a house.

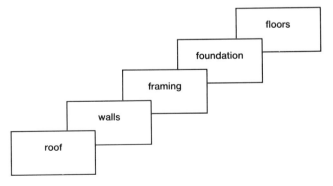

3. Compare the Roof and Framing cards. The framing must go up earlier to support the roof, so interchange the card order to:
   Walls
   Framing
   Roof
   Foundation
   Floors
4. Compare the Roof and Foundation cards. The foundation must be laid first since the rest of the structure must rest on it so interchange the order of these two cards and arrive at:
   Walls
   Framing
   Foundation
   Roof
   Floors
5. Compare the Roof and Floors cards. The roof must be erected to protect the floors, so do not exchange the order of these last two cards.

The order after the first round of comparisons is shown in Figure 5-3.

Continue making all the comparisons, exchanging the order of the component that should be completed first. The final order is shown in Figure 5-4. The Foundation card bubbled up to the top and became the component that must be built first.

Now the tree can be redrawn to reflect the order of constructing a house:

Figure 5-3. Order of cards at end of Round 1.

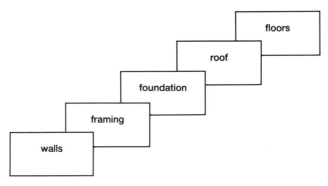

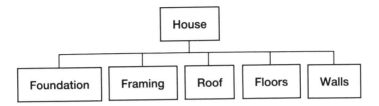

The tree now not only shows which components make up the complete house, it also shows the left-to-right order in which the components should be assembled to construct the house: build the foundation first, then the framing, and so on.

This same technique will be used later in this book to show how to design from the top down and then organize and write from the bottom up manuscripts of all formats and lengths.

Block Diagrams

Whereas the tree shows the overall top-to-bottom construction relationship of an object or a process, the block diagram illustrates the interaction of components on the same level, i.e., how components of equal importance react with each other. Most business communication does not involve writing about things that are static, such as a painting. Like life, business writing is about things that move and change, for example, a motor driving a gear or a medicine reacting to the chemicals in a person's body.

The block diagram is one of the simplest of the visuals used in

Figure 5-4. Final sorted order of cards.

walls

floors

roof

framing

foundation

business writing. It is easy to construct and understand, it is attractive in layout, and its visual character helps readers remember the concept.

Because the block diagram is so widely used and is familiar to most readers, it's an excellent visual to use to explain how something dynamic—electrical, physical, psychological, or mechanical—functions. The diagram is simple to construct with word processors and eliminates considerable redundant text when compared to a strictly textual explanation of a function. Block diagrams also add much-needed white space to a page. Since they are visual, they help readers understand and better remember the concepts they are utilized to explain.

The following block diagram depicts a television receiver:

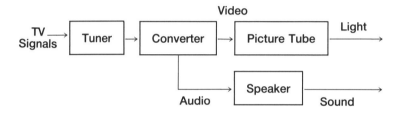

The tuner in the TV set selects the specific station that the viewer elects to watch, rejecting all the other signals. The converter changes these electrical signals from the tuner into two types of electrical signals: video (picture) and audio (sound). The video signal paints the multicolor picture on the picture tube, line by line, converting it to light for the viewer. At the same time, in parallel, the audio signal is amplified and then used to drive the speaker, delivering sound in synchronism with the TV picture so that the proper sound is delivered by the speaker in synchronism with the performers' actions and lip movements.

As you can see, a block diagram is not a physical representation of the equipment. There is little or no correlation between the actual physical size and/or shape of the TV set components and the blocks that represent them. A block diagram is a functional diagram that illustrates not how things look, but how the components interact with each other.

Guidelines for Block Diagrams

■ *Limit the number of blocks.* Use no more than ten to twelve blocks in any single block diagram. Nothing can overwhelm and discourage your reader more than to be confronted with a maze of twenty to fifty functional blocks on a single sheet of paper, with crisscrossing lines.

The mind cannot grapple with such a huge mountain of information in parallel. It's like trying to read an entire page of a book at once. Break a complex diagram down into several simple block diagrams.

- *Use "A" size paper.* Using A size (8½ by 11 inches) paper disciplines you to use no more than about ten blocks in a diagram.

- *Use conventional flow.* Observe the conventional directions of information flow: left to right or top to bottom.

- Reduce the *"muddle" factor.* To reduce the muddle factor, minimize the number of interconnecting lines so you show only major actions and interactions.

- *Use functional names.* Give each block a short, functional name of no more than three or four meaningful words. Don't use "Amplifier A"; instead, designate it by its descriptive name, "Audio Amplifier."

- *Use consistent labels.* Make sure that inputs and outputs to and from different diagrams have exactly the same names. An input signal should not be designated "data input" on one diagram and "digital input" for the same signal on an interconnecting diagram.

Schematic/Logic Diagrams

Schematic/logic diagrams detail each component in a device and show how they interconnect (Figure 5-5).

Line Drawings

Line drawings comprise lines drawn to illustrate how an object looks (Figure 5-6). They are excellent substitutes for a photograph and often show details much better than a photograph can. Cutaways can omit extraneous detail and give readers a peek inside a piece of equipment to illustrate how it functions.

For anything but the simplest line drawings, a skilled illustrator is needed. Unless you have the proper artistic talent, turn the task over to an artist and either sketch it out or verbally describe the type of visual you need. Work closely with the illustrator to make sure he or she provides you with the views, the detail, and the overall concept you require. You can then concentrate on writing the text that complements and explains how the object depicted in the visual operates.

Relatively simple line drawings can be created by modern word processing or graphic programs that operate on a personal computer. A big advantage of using a PC to provide these (and other) visuals is

Figure 5-5. Schematic diagram: components of an electronic submodule.

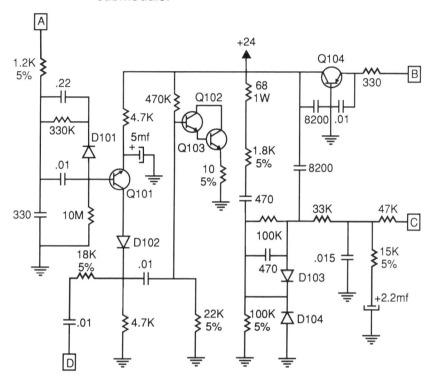

that they can be stored on disk, recalled later, easily modified, and printed out using standard printing techniques, and they can be delivered in final form to a publisher, stored on a floppy disk.

Line drawings created by an illustrator are usually costly and time-consuming to make, but if you need to depict precisely how a complex object looks, you must use either a line drawing or a photograph.

Line drawings can be constructed either from a photo, engineering drawings, observation of the object itself, or completely from the writer's and illustrator's collective imaginations, as often happens with proposals.

Photographs

To illustrate precisely how an object looks on the outside, nothing is superior to a photograph (Figure 5-7). Photographs are inexpensive to

Figure 5-6. Line drawing of a power system.

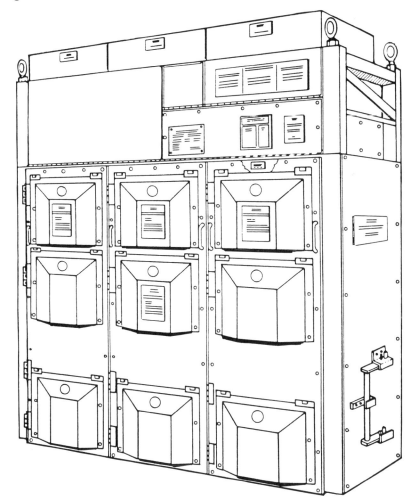

make, and they provide minute detail. Even amateurs, given the proper camera, film, and lighting, can produce a useable photo. Photographs are generally expensive to reproduce in a document, however.

Free photographs are available not only from within your own company but also from a number of other sources. Large corporations, public relations firms, and others will give you photographs and the permission to use them in your manuscripts as long as you credit the donor in your publication.

Figure 5-7.   Photograph of calculators (precisely what your eyes see).

Government organizations, such as the Library of Congress, supply photos for a small fee. The library's address for photos is:

Library of Congress
Prints and Photographs Division
Madison Building, Room LM 339
Washington, D.C. 20540 (202) 287-6394

Observe the following special precautions when using photographs:

- Use glossy 8- by 10-inch photographs, although 5- by 7-inch glossies are acceptable. Photos from instant-developing cameras are usually not acceptable.
- If you mail photos, use stiff cardboard or something else in the envelope to protect them. Stamp or print DO NOT BEND on the mailing envelope.
- Do not fold, paper clip, or staple photographs.
- Write the caption and figure number on the back of each photograph using a self-adhesive label or on a transparent overlay. Do not write directly on the back with a pen, or you will mar the photo.

Line drawings and photographs are not interchangeable. Photos do not show the inner workings of a device, as line drawings do. Moreover, light and shadow often obscure the inner details of objects. And, of course, you must have access to the object to photograph it. Although line drawings show more detail, they often cost ten to as much as a hundred times more than a photograph of comparable detail. Sometimes governing specifications require that only line drawings be used since photographs cannot be microfilmed for archival purposes.

Exploded Views

Exploded views are so designated because they look like a photograph snapped when the device is in the process of exploding apart. They thus show the various components that make up a device in the proper scale (Figure 5-8).

An exploded view is actually a drawing of the device partially disassembled, showing enough detail so that readers can understand how to disassemble and reassemble the device. The exploded view also illustrates the parts in sufficient detail so that the individual parts can be identified and replaced if they malfunction. Text is often generated to accompany the exploded view and to list the sequential steps and procedures required to disassemble and reassemble the device.

Exploded views are expensive to create but a necessity for some types of documents. They are commonly used, for example, in instruction booklets for home appliances.

Graphs

Graphs are most widely used for presenting data—for example, to show how one or more continuous (or extrapolated) variable(s) change with

Figure 5-8.   Exploded view of a brush assembly.

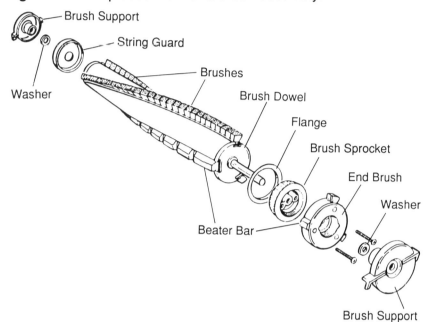

Brush Support

String Guard

Brushes

Washer

Brush Dowel

Flange

Brush Sprocket

End Brush

Washer

Beater Bar

Brush Support

respect to another variable(s) or to show trends or minimums or maximums. They provide you with a picture that is easy to grasp. For example, a 50 percent drop in the price of a personal computer over a three-year period is conveyed much more dramatically in a graph than in words in the text.

Line Graphs

One of the most popular of all graphs is the line graph (Figure 5-9). Although their data presentation capability is not as precise as it is for tables, communicating trends or relationships is often more important than showing exact data points. The line graph is ideal for showing a dramatic side-by-side comparison of two variables: the independent on the horizontal or X-axis and the dependent on the vertical or Y-axis. If more than three lines are used, the graph can be difficult to interpret. Three-dimensional (X-Y-Z) graphs are used occasionally to illustrate complex relationships.

The following guidelines will help you use this type of visual effectively:

Figure 5-9. Typical line graph.

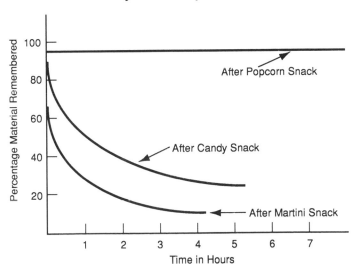

- To emphasize a curve or a trend, choose a vertical scale such that the slope of the curve will be 45 degrees or greater. The idea of movement or trend is best emphasized by the steepness of the line and is minimized by flatness.
- If your graph contains only one curve, add another dimension by coding or cross-hatching the area under the curve.
- Label all coordinates simply.
- Use a minimum number of grid lines and plotted lines so that the curved lines stand out.
- Graduate the horizontal axis in equal increments; do the same for the vertical axis.
- Label curves directly rather than using a key.
- Don't run the curves to the ends of the grids; leave a 10 to 15 percent space all around.

Bar Graphs

Bar graphs (Figure 5-10) are a pictorial method of displaying tabular data when no mathematical relationship exists among the variables. They are particularly useful for dramatically illustrating relationships among different sets of data. Bar graphs give a quick picture and are

Figure 5-10.   Typical bar graph.

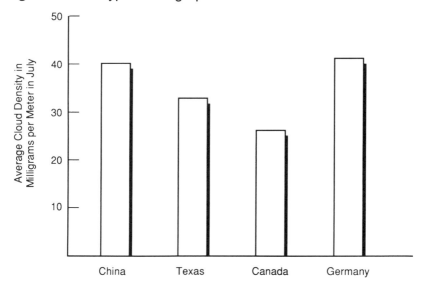

much easier to make comparisons with than a pie chart. If the bars are too short or too long, however, they lose their effectiveness.

Clarity is best served by separating the individual bars. Choosing the scale carefully and using bars of the same width and the same spacing makes them attractive and easy to understand. The bars may be plotted vertically—for presenting the types of data that people expect to see vertically, such as temperature and weight—or horizontally— suitable for distance, time, speed, and so on. Shading or cross-hatching the bars adds another dimension of information, such as changes with time or grouping by categories.

Bar graphs can also be used to show the different portions of items that make up the whole. The bars can be divided up into lengths according to their percentages of the whole. (The sum of the bars should be 100 percent.)

Pie Charts

Pie charts present data as wedge-shaded sections of a circle; they provide an easy-to-understand and dramatic picture of the parts that constitute a whole (Figure 5-11). A pie chart provides a quick comparison of the relative sizes of the items. It shows proportions and the relative

Figure 5-11. Pie chart.

Typical Use of Family Auto

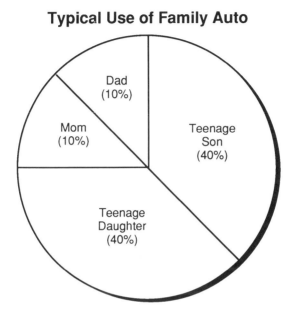

size of related quantities of items in a static situation. It does not show trends or changes. Pie charts are best used when the relationships among percentages of a whole are more important than the amount of the whole.

A pie chart should not be cut up into too many slices; the maximum should be six. A pie chart doesn't work well when its wedges are many and of small amounts. The smallest wedge should be greater than 2 percent of the whole pie.

To make the relative sizes as clear as possible, begin at the twelve o'clock position with the largest slice and sequence the slices clockwise from the largest to the smallest. Keep all labels horizontal. Remember that a pie chart is not accurate; it can't convey the difference between, say, 27 percent and 31 percent. If accuracy is required, label the percentages on or near each slice.

For emphasis, shade individual elements or cross-hatch them to code the various parts. Make sure the various slices are labeled with their categories, as well as the percentages of the whole they represent. And double-check to make sure that all of the slices add up to 100 percent.

Tables

Use tables when:

- A point can be made more clearly than if you used only text.
- The data in the table are not duplicated in the accompanying text.
- Conveying exact quantities of data is important.
- Putting the data in the text would take at least three times as much page space.

Although tables condense information, they are less desirable than graphs since readers must try to formulate a picture in their minds based on the numbers in the table. Nevertheless, if you must present numerical data with a high degree of accuracy and a graph won't work, you can make your table as clear as possible by setting it off from the text with adequate space, using footnotes to clarify entries, restricting it to a single page if possible, and discussing the data in the accompanying text to help with their interpretation.

Informal Tables

An informal table lists items in vertical order for visual clarity and quick reference. It has no lines or ruled forms and can be placed in the middle of text. The following informal table shows the percentage concentrations of various chemicals in smog:

Oxygen	4%
Nitrogen	6%
Carbon dioxide	90%

Informal tables must be brief and simple. They are not identified by a table number and normally do not have a title.

Formal Tables

Large quantities of dense information, such as statistics, percentages, results, or quantities, etc., may be difficult to understand in a prose format. A solution is to extract the data and present them in a table for quick comparison and ease of understanding.

A formal table requires a table number, a table name, and lines to clarify the presentation. Column headings identify the nature of the

Figure 5-12. Table format.

Table Number and Name			
		Multiple-Column Caption	
Stub Caption	*Column Caption*	*Subcaption*	*Subcaption*
1 Heading 1	Data	More Data	And More
2 Heading 2	Data		
3 Heading 3	Data		
4 Heading 4	Data		

data and the units of measurement (such as ounces, feet, or percentages) (Figure 5-12).

The use of a formal table eliminates the cumbersome repetition of units. The tabular arrangement helps readers to compare data easily and quickly.

As a guideline, when four or more sets of data are to be presented, it's best to use a formal table. To prepare effective formal tables:

- Leave generous amounts of white space.
- Align columns on the decimal point.
- Clearly label all columns. Don't overabbreviate, and don't use too many columns or rows.
- Use decimals, not fractions.
- Try to keep the table to one column width if you're writing for a periodical.
- Don't leave cells in a table blank. If no figures are available, use a dash (—).

Illustration Quality

Authors are required to deliver illustrations with a manuscript that are clear and in rough-draft form—whether they are for internal company use or for external publication. Most art departments and publishers redraw the art to meet their own standards and requirements; however, some outside periodical and book publishers require that an author supply camera-ready art. If this is the case, you'll probably have to hire an illustrator, at your expense. An inexpensive option is to limit the majority of your visuals to those that can be drawn by computer graphic programs or illustrations that can be donated by companies that are anxious to see their names in print and will eagerly supply the material you need. (Be sure to credit the companies.)

Another possible source of visuals is the use of clip art, available at no charge from a number of vendors. This wide variety of art can be obtained from clip-art books at public libraries or by purchasing clip-art books from art stores and some publishers. Clip art is also available in many software programs.

Color illustrations are costly and should be discouraged for most professional books. Obviously there are cases where color is a necessity, but any usage should be cleared with the publisher.

6

Principles of Good Writing

> The greatest merit of style, of course, is to have words
> disappear into thoughts.
>
> —Nathaniel Hawthorne

"My father was a man of great intellectual energy," said Woodrow Wilson. "My best training came from him. I carried with me everything I wrote to him. He would make me read it aloud. Every now and then he would stop me with: 'What do you mean by that?' he'd ask. I would tell him, and of course, in doing so I would express myself more simply than I had on paper. 'Why didn't you say so?' he would go on. 'Don't shoot at your meaning with birdshot and hit the whole countryside; shoot with a rifle at the thing you have to say.' "

This chapter heeds this wise counsel. You'll learn what good writing is and how to achieve it with rifle shots by writing with clarity, precision, brevity, and the force of logic. The basic principles of good writing, concentrating on business applications, will be covered here.

The great masters of style, William Strunk, Jr., and E. B. White, wrote in their *The Elements of Style*, "Vigorous writing is concise. A sentence should contain no unnecessary words, a paragraph no unnecessary sentences, for the same reason that a drawing should have no unnecessary lines and a machine no unnecessary parts. This requires not that the writer make all of his sentences short, or that he avoid all

details and treat his subjects only in outline, but that every word tell."
No one could have said it any better.

Identifying Good Writing

Good writing effectively communicates what the writer has to say, with
a minimum of effort on the reader's part. It is characterized by logically
organized material, use of the active voice, good grammar and correct
spelling, short sentences and paragraphs, and short words.

Good writing is invisible. In his *Collected Essays*, George Orwell
likened it to a window pane: "The less you're aware of it, the better."
Good writing, in other words, helps your reader easily understand what
you've written but does not make obvious which specific techniques
you've used to attain these effects. Properly used, these techniques are
totally transparent to your readers.

How We Read

First let's look at the basic manner in which we read. The more mental
energy it takes to dig the meanings out of words, sentences, and paragraphs, the less energy readers have left to interpret what they read,
and the more likely they will quit in exhaustion, frustration, irritation,
or despair.

When we read business-oriented material, we use energy in three
basic ways:

1. To understand the words
2. To understand how the words relate to each other to form pictures, thoughts
3. To understand the complex concepts and ideas described by the
   words and the accompanying visuals

When we read fiction and most popular nonfiction, we use mental
energy only on the first two ways listed above. Business writing, however, adds a third and more difficult aspect: comprehending the complex concepts.

If you use short, simple, concrete words, you make the first step
easy. A variety of short, well-constructed sentences makes the second
task effortless. That eliminates two-thirds of the effort of reading, so

your readers can concentrate all their energy on understanding the complex concepts.

Words

The basic element of writing is the word. But the 500 most used English words have about 14,000 dictionary definitions, for an average of 28 meanings per word. And words can form radically different shades of meaning in different people's minds. For example, *house* can conjure up a picture ranging from a tiny, rundown shack to a mansion. You can see the importance of using the proper word.

Abstract words, (e.g., *courage, love, problem, terrific*) refer to ideas, acts, qualities, and conditions. Concrete words refer to specific persons, places, objects, and acts (e.g., *house, Tom Jones, golf ball, taste*). They are easier to understand than abstract words because they create clear pictures in readers' minds.

How do you identify concrete words? To test for concreteness, can you:

- Feel it?
- See it?
- Hear it?
- Taste it?
- Smell it?

Most important, does the word invoke one, and only one, clear picture in your mind and in readers' minds? If you set your words in concrete, you'll have a solid foundation for your manuscript. In writing, as in design, use only the essential parts needed to do the job.

Groups of words (phrases and sentences) modify and clarify the intrinsic meaning of individual words. Words should be used to sharpen the focus of the picture they are intended to create. "Man" gives a somewhat fuzzy, indefinite picture. "Fat man" focuses the picture a little more. "Short, swarthy, grossly fat man" sharply focuses the image that the words convey. The more concrete the words are, the sharper and the more in focus will be the picture they create.

The Curse of Big Words

Bertrand Russell stated in his essay "How I Write": "Big men write little words, little men write big words."

Written ideas and concepts are difficult enough to understand without a writer's complicating them even more by trying to show off his or her vocabulary. When you write a long word like *matriculate,* your readers must expend the time and the energy needed to translate that longer word into its simple equivalent, *enroll,* before they can see the image or action.

You should write to express, not to impress. Even the most complex ideas can be presented by simple (three syllable or less) words. Some of the most brilliant scientists of all time (Darwin, Pasteur, and Madame Curie are examples) explained their complex concepts in words so simple that the public could understand and appreciate the significance of their discoveries. Undoubtedly their clear writing contributed as much to their fame as did their discoveries.

Word Order

It's not only the words you use but also the word order that's important. Words in sentences must be arranged so they can mean only what is intended. In the English language, changing the word order changes the meaning:

Man bites snake.
Snake bites man.

The proper word order is required to paint the precise picture you want.

Another important aspect of helping your readers understand is *consecutiveness:* things happen in a given order:

Add 1 liter of water to the solution, shake vigorously for 10 seconds, and then add 1 gram of KCl."

Using the proper sequence makes an idea easier to follow.

Still, words are not substitutes for thoughts. You must group words together to form a sentence. But no sentence, no matter which words you use, is any better than the thought behind it.

A sentence should carry only a single meaning. The basic pattern of a sentence is:

Subject	*Verb*	*Object*
Thing $\longrightarrow$	Doing $\longrightarrow$	Result
Man $\longrightarrow$	Tosses $\longrightarrow$	Horseshoe

Using the proper words in this basic SVO (subject-verb-object) order make writing easier to understand because the active voice describes the natural sequence in which things happen. First you "see" the man, then the tossing motion, and then the horseshoe (the object being thrown). The active voice emphasizes the subject (man) and subordinates the object (horseshoe). The SVO usually uses fewer words for sentence completeness.

"The horseshoe was tossed by the man" is a backward construction, using the passive voice. It jerks your mind out of gear because it's not the natural order in which the event occurred. First your mind focuses on the horseshoe (what is it doing there?), then on the passive "was tossed," and finally on the "man," the most important part of the sentence. You have to unscramble it in your mind and wrestle it back into the proper order before you can understand it, a process that wastes mental energy.

To make such a sentence give a more complete picture, add a few more descriptive words:

The tall, slender man tossed the horseshoe to ring the peg.

Words must be arranged in the proper grammatical form to carry the right meaning. A study of twenty top writers (ten fiction and ten nonfiction), conducted by Francis Christensen of the University of Southern California, found that over 75 percent of all the sentences in their writing used SVO order ("snake bites man"). Another 23 percent of the sentences began with a short adverbial opener, such as *however, therefore,* and *nevertheless,* followed by the basic SVO sentence. Thus, the SVO and the adverbial plus SVO were used an impressive 98.5 percent of the time by professional writers. If you want to be understood easily, use the common SVO order in most of your sentences.

Vocabulary

We read in terms of words, and we understand words within the limits of our vocabulary. Unless your message is contained within the identical area of the vocabulary that you and your readers share (as shown below) there is no communication. Moreover, the words in the message must mean the same to both you and the reader.

Readers who are confronted by big or unfamiliar words must pause in their reading, consult their memories or a dictionary, and translate the word into a more common one that they understand. This process

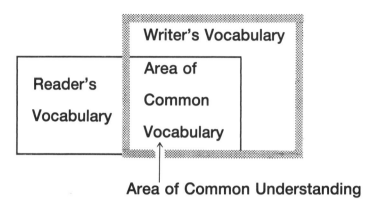

Area of Common Understanding

requires extra effort, it can interrupt the chain of thought that you are trying to create, and it can frustrate and discourage readers.

A larger vocabulary isn't necessary for effective communication. An estimated 1,000 words cover about 85 percent of a writer's requirements on all ordinary subjects. You can certainly do most of your writing without resorting to long, abstract, indefinite, or fuzzy words. If you use as many of the 1,000 basic words as you can in place of complex words or jargon, your writing will be easier to read and to understand.

Grammar

Words must be arranged in the proper grammatical form to convey the correct meaning. Grammar embraces:

Phonology: Study of meaningful sounds
Word forms: Singular, plural, tense, gender
Syntax: Arranging words in a meaningful sequence
Semantics: Science of meaning

Proper grammar must be used not only to avoid misunderstanding but also because your readers will notice and be disturbed by poor grammar. Their minds are distracted and jerked away from understanding the intent of your manuscript. Grammatical errors alter your writing so it is no longer transparent, distracting readers' attention away from the primary purpose of your writing: communicating information.

Spelling

When your manuscript is sprinkled with misspelled words, your readers' minds are diverted from focusing on the content. When people read a document full of typos, other errors, and misspelled words, they also begin to distrust the accuracy of the content, the ideas, the data—everything associated with the document. Moreover, misspelled words distract readers from what you are trying to say and make reading more difficult.

Of the approximately 20,000 commonly used words, only 1 percent are consistently misspelled. Of these 200, the 50 that cause the most trouble are listed, left to right, in order of difficulty:

grammar	*argument*	*surprise*	*achieve*
anoint	*definitely*	*separate*	*desirable*
development	*existence*	*pronunciation*	*occasion*
assistant	*repetition*	*privilege*	*dependent*
irresistible	*consensus*	*accommodate*	*occurrence*
conscience	*commitment*	*embarrass*	*allotted*
indispensable	*liaison*	*proceed*	*harass*
perseverance	*ecstasy*	*antiquated*	*insistent*
exhilarate	*vacuum*	*ridiculous*	*nickel*
oscillate	*tyrannous*	*drunkenness*	*dissension*
connoisseur	*sacrilegious*	*battalion*	*prerogative*
iridescent	*inadvertent*	*genealogy*	*vilify*
inoculate	*dilettante*		

Study and then be especially careful with these words, make sure they're all in your computer spelling program, and you'll have a good start.

Providing Continuity to Words

Sentences

Short sentences and paragraphs have been proved to be more effective in communicating ideas than their longer equivalents. A reader attempts to comprehend an entire sentence in one gulp, looking ahead to the period or other ending punctuation (the rest period) before pausing momentarily. Short sentences and paragraphs permit spacing of ideas for easier comprehension. And short words are usually concrete. If a sentence runs on too long, stop it with a period or a semicolon. As sentences become longer, relationships among words become murky. By the time your readers get to the end of a long sentence, they may have forgotten what was at the beginning. To write snappy sentences:

- Put the main message at the front of the sentence.
- If your statement has to be qualified, do that in the next short sentence.
- If a sentence runs on too long, stop it with a period or semicolon.

Paragraphs

A paragraph is a sentence or group of sentences that expresses and develops one major idea. It groups together sentences that confirm the same topic and combine to form a thought unit. Minds are geared to reading and understanding a single idea. Readers feel that when they finish a paragraph, the idea has been completely presented and they deserve a momentary pause before tackling the next idea or paragraph. Long paragraphs and complex thoughts tire readers.

Readers of business writing can grasp material most readily when it is presented in units of 75 to 200 words. With an average of 10 words per typed line, that allows about 7.5 to 20 lines per paragraph. Don't take this guideline as gospel and feel that all paragraphs must fit between these limits. These numbers are averages—a way to check your writing along the way. Use brief paragraphs to convey less important ideas and longer paragraphs for more important ideas.

The most effective way to introduce the idea that the paragraph is to cover is to use a topic sentence as the first sentence in the paragraph. Writing experts claim that using topic sentences cuts the length of manuscripts (and the attendant writing time) by 25 to 50 percent without sacrificing content. The topic sentence indicates the direction an idea is to take and helps to guide readers to the central purpose of the paragraph. It leads readers through the development of the main idea so that they reach the conclusion that the writer intended.

The topic sentence isn't always placed at the beginning of the paragraph. It can come at the end if the paragraph is developed by induction. And if the writer considers the main point vital, he or she may emphasize it at both the beginning and the end of the paragraph. Wherever the topic sentence is placed, it should dominate the paragraph. The rest of the paragraph should serve mainly to develop it.

The topic sentence is often followed by one or more subtopic sentences that develop, clarify, and prove the thesis of the topic sentence. Facts, statistics, or quotations from experts can be included as part of the proof and be used to form the subtopics. Without this proof, the reader will wonder about the basis for the idea.

The last sentence in the paragraph may be a conclusion, a call to action, or a transitional phrase that links the next topic or idea.

Transitions

Transitions—words, synonyms, phrases, and sometimes sentences—are important literary devices. They are bridges that link paragraphs, thoughts, and ideas together. They provide continuity so readers can move smoothly from one topic to the next without feeling a jolt in continuity. Continuity can be established by a recognizable flow of thought. Recognition is helped by repetition of words, especially key words, and phrases. Transitions connect what has been said with what is about to be said.

Commonly Used Transitions

- Time: later, the next time, finally, next, concurrently, after
- Place: in the next room, farther down the hall, at our plant in Oregon
- Piling up of detail: and, also, furthermore, in addition, moreover, besides
- Contrast: but, however, though, although, nonetheless, yet
- Illustration: for example, to illustrate, in particular, for instance
- Cause and effect: thus, therefore, in conclusion, as a consequence, as a result, consequently, subsequently
- Comparison: in a similar way, likewise, similarly, here again, consequently
- Concession: although, even though, since, though
- Summary: to sum up, in brief, in short
- Repetition: in other words, that is, as has been stated

Punctuation

Punctuation is the written equivalent of the rhythm and emphasis in speech. It takes the place of the rise and fall of the voice, the pauses and emphasis in speech, and gestures. The major function of punctuation is to make writing clearer and easier to read. Punctuation helps express, question, emphasize, surprise, and conclude.

When we speak, listeners learn as much from the way we speak as they learn from the words we use. We gesture, screw up our face, raise or lower our voice, pause, speak fast or slow, high or low, use our hands, eyebrows, our facial expressions to add emphasis to words. It's quite a challenge to use punctuation to emulate spoken words and gestures.

Commas

About half of the total number of punctuation marks used in writing are commas. A comma separates words or phrases to avoid confusion and ambiguity. It's the main device by which grouping of words, phrases, and clauses is indicated. The comma gives a short pause to illustrate and emphasize this separation. Use a comma where you would normally pause in a conversation.

I believe that the comma is the most abused of all the punctuation marks, and it is abused more in omission than in commission. The meaning of a sentence can be totally altered by adding or changing the position of the comma. Consider an example:

The talented actress, Margaret Anglin, once watched the famous Mrs. Fiske do a wonderfully dramatic performance that impressed her so greatly that she scribbled a note on her program and sent it to Mrs. Fiske backstage. The note read: "Margaret Anglin thinks Mrs. Fiske is the greatest actress in America."

During the next intermission the note was returned to Miss Anglin with two commas added. It now read: "Margaret Anglin, thinks Mrs. Fiske, is the greatest actress in America."

Other Punctuation Marks

▪ The *period* signifies the end of a sentence; it is equivalent to a longer pause by a speaker. Try to avoid using periods in abbreviations; they confuse readers, who mistakenly conclude that they've reached the end of a sentence. Instead, spell out the words. (An exception is commonly used abbreviations such as *etc.*)

Writing experts agree that the period is not used often enough in business writing. It should be used more frequently to end sentences sooner.

▪ The *semicolon* is sort of a half-period; it gives a pause halfway in length between the comma and the period. The semicolon is optional; you don't have to use it, and in fact most great writers seldom do. Yet one renowned writer, George Will, loves it: "It is almost always a greater pleasure to come across a semicolon than a period. . . . You get a pleasant little feeling of expectancy, there is more to come, read on, it will get clearer."

• The *colon* introduces a list of details or an explanation. It is equivalent to a speaker's gesture or a lift of the eyebrow.

• The *exclamation point* is the written equivalent of a speaker's emphasizing a point with a raised voice or a gesture.

• The *question mark* takes the place of a voice being raised at the end of a question.

In spite of all the confusing and sometimes vague rules about punctuation, the best guideline for proper punctuation is common sense: Forget what the grammarians say about periods, commas, and other punctuation. If you feel that putting a stop or a pause in a specific place in your sentence will clarify it for your reader, do so. And if you find you're using too many commas in your sentences, perhaps your sentences are too long and confusing. Shorten or reshape them to make them easier to understand.

Like all other tools, punctuation marks can be overused. Too many stops produce a jerky style, hindering readers from understanding your writing.

Don't Overdo It

These techniques will lose their effectiveness if you overdo them. Using only one or two sentences for every paragraph all through your document or ten-word "Dick and Jane and Spot" sentences will distract readers from understanding the message you want to convey. Your task is to use the techniques of good writing to communicate smoothly, without readers' becoming aware of how you achieve your goal. The techniques of writing should be invisible.

The Retention Curve

One extremely important aspect of the manner in which the mind works is illustrated in Figure 6-1. This retention curve is valid for all people,

Figure 6-1. Retention curve.

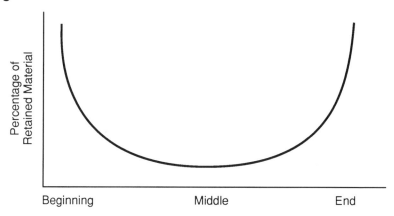

Section of Article, Book, Report, Movie, Speech, etc.

of all cultures, regardless of education. It's a fundamental fact of human nature. Stated simply, the curve illustrates that:

> **The mind remembers best what it experiences, hears, and reads *first* and *last.***

This fact holds true for a book, a movie, a speech, a poem, an article, your life's experiences . . . whatever you see, hear, or read.

That's why the HEY! YOU! and SO! sections of your document are so important. Your reader will best remember the beginning and ending sections. That's why the summary and conclusion of your manuscript are worth your best efforts.

The same phenomenon holds true for both sentences and paragraphs. That readers best remember the first and last parts of sentences and paragraphs explains why the topic sentence is so important. The final sentence of your paragraph should be a sort of conclusion, leaving your readers with the feeling of having been introduced to a concept in the first sentence and ending with understanding the idea put forth in the topic sentence.

Keep the retention curve in mind when you want to emphasize one or more points. Put the most important points in the first part of your writing—in the first paragraphs and first sentences of paragraphs—and at the beginnings and endings of sentences. Save some of your best writing for the conclusion.

You can use the retention curve to conceal poor data or meager results by burying this bad information, which you must include for completeness, in the middle of the document. A strong opening paragraph can often negate the bad information that may have been created by the data in the middle.

Anecdotes

Anecdotes are another effective method of leading into a topic and making a point at the same time. We all like to peek into other people's lives, and we learn much by observing them. Anecdotes also add a much needed degree of informality to pedantic periodicals.

Even though your manuscript may be business oriented, don't forget that businesses are run by people, not machines. And your writing will be read and enjoyed by people, not by a computer. So people, and their stories, belong in your writing.

Although anecdotes may not have much application in some business publications such as proposals and reports, they certainly deserve a place in articles and books. (Note that this chapter begins with an anecdote.) To be effective, they should relate directly to your topic by illustrating it, expanding on it, introducing it, or making a point. They should not be dragged in simply to entertain; they should be an essential part of your presentation.

Direct quotations from well-known people or experts in your profession are another effective method of introducing a topic or of making a point. One study, by the Kentucky Department of Communication, found that readers expressed a preference for direct quotations rather than paraphrased statements.

Readability

Readability Index

Over the years a number of communication experts have developed various readability formulas that provide a quantitative evaluation of a written document showing the relative ease of reading it. By using the number of words in a sentence and the number of syllables in the words, this formula comes up with a number called the Readability Index. It relates to the number of years of education a person should have to be able to read and understand a specific piece of writing.

The Readability Index of John Steinbeck's novels is 7; that of the *Reader's Digest* is 8; and the *Wall Street Journal, Time,* and *Newsweek* are judged a 10. This means that the sentence length and number of syllables per sentence in *The Reader's Digest,* for example, are written so they can be read and understood by a person having an eighth-grade education, and only a tenth-grade education is required for the *Wall Street Journal* and *Time* and *Newsweek* magazines. Writing communicates best when the readability level is slightly below the comprehension level of the average reader so readers can enjoy the prose without having to strain for meaning or deal with long sentences.

By its nature, technology and business writing is a little more complex and tends toward a specially educated audience. A Readability Index of about 12 is satisfactory for most technology and business writing, but 10 is a better standard to strive for. In some military manuals, a Readability Index of 8 to 9 is required.

Fog Index

The Fog Index, developed by Robert Gunning and based on the contents of long words and sentence lengths, includes a factor that relates it to the approximate number of years of schooling needed to understand the prose. The higher the Fog Index is, the more difficult the material is to read.*

You can calculate the Fog Index with a writing sample of at least 100 words:

1. Count the average number of words per sentence, treating independent clauses as separate sentences.
2. Count the number of polysyllables (words of three syllables or more) per 100 words. Do not count capitalized words, combinations of short, easy words (such as *peoplepower*) and verbs that are made into three syllables by adding *-es* or *-ed.*
3. Add the average number of words per sentence to the polysyllable count and multiply the sum by 0.4. Ignore digits after the decimal point.

*R. Gunning, *The Techniques of Clear Writing* (New York: McGraw-Hill, 1968).

If you end up with a number over 17, you are in too deep a fog. Work your way down to 10 or less.

To see how the index works, here is an example:

> In spite of the tendency of most scientific writers to use big words, even the most complex concepts can be explained in simple words. [24 words, 2 polysyllables] It doesn't take big words to explain big concepts. [9 words, 0 polysyllables] For example, why should a writer say that "as the temperature is elevated to the vicinity of 100 degrees Centigrade, the condition of the water becomes vaporous"? [27 words, 6 polysyllables] How much simpler it is to say, "At 100 degrees Centigrade the water turns to steam." [16 words, 0 polysyllables]

The paragraph has a total of 76 words and 5 sentences, for an average of 15 words per sentence, and 8 polysyllables, or about 10 polysyllables per 100 words. Calculate the Fog Index:

$$\text{Fog Index} = 0.4(15 + 10) = 10$$

A tenth-grade education is required to understand the passage.

If you find yourself shaking your head when you read something, pause for a moment and analyze why. Did the author use long sentences? Are the sentences filled with polysyllable words that confuse your mind instead of explaining the idea? And when you read something that is easy to understand, pause a moment also. Did the author use short and varied-length sentences and simple words? Are the thoughts logically organized so that one follows another in the proper order? Look back at the example paragraph.

Isn't the second statement in each pair much easier to read and understand? It contains the same information but in fewer and less complex words.

A Warning

Don't take these rules for sentence length and number of polysyllables as gospel. They are intended only as rough guidelines to help you check and keep a rein on your writing. They are, however, very useful to help you from becoming too pompous and long-winded.

Using Lean Prose

What the Writer Said	What the Writer Should Have Said
The purpose of this report is . . .	This report describes . . .
This report is submitted to . . .	This report sums up . . .
In order to complete . . .	To complete . . . ("In order" can be left out of all writing.)
It is recommended that the procedure should be . . .	The procedure should be . . . (Watch out for "It . . . that" constructions; they waste a lot of words).
In accordance with . . .	Per . . .
As defined in . . .	Per . . .
Shall have the capability of expanding . . .	Shall expand . . .
The VCR shall be tested per . . .	Test the VCR per . . .
Due to the fact that . . .	Since . . .
Demonstrates that there is . . .	Shows . . .
During such time . . .	While . . .
If the developments are such that . . .	If . . .
Make an approximation as to how . . .	Estimate . . .
Reduced to basic essentials . . .	Simplified . . .
Would seem to suggest . . .	Suggests
For the purpose of . . .	For; to . . .
Is designed to be . . .	Is . . .
In close proximity . . .	Close to; near . . .
Subsequent to . . .	After . . .
In the event that . . .	If . . .
In order to . . .	To . . .
Involves the use of . . .	Employs; uses . . .

7

The Library and On-Line Databases

A man will turn over half a library to make one book.

—Samuel Johnson

Research, the process of getting facts and opinions from the world outside yourself and evaluating them for your own purposes, is the foundation of nonfiction writing. When you're working on a manuscript, you may have to do research to determine what others in your profession have accomplished on similar topics.

The best repositories of knowledge are libraries and commercial on-line data banks. Nearly everything you want to know has been printed—somewhere, sometime. But sometimes the sheer magnitude of what's available makes it difficult to locate precisely what you're looking for. This chapter will show you where to look, what to look for, and how to find the exact information you need in the most expeditious manner.

What Researchers Need to Know

All researchers need to know:

1. Where to look
2. How long to look

This chapter shows you where to look. The "how long" is up to you. Knowing where to look, and what to look for, can save you much valuable time. Skilled librarians and abstracters spend hundreds of thousands of hours yearly categorizing, cataloging, indexing, referencing, and abstracting the articles and books that are published each year.

Books are the most important reference for research, but they are often out of date. Periodicals contain the most up-to-date information but generally do not cover subjects in adequate depth. Contacting experts, either by telephone or by mail, is another method of obtaining the latest information, but this is often time-consuming, and establishing contact may be difficult. To be thorough, you need to know how to utilize all possible types of research sources. (You can refer to Appendix A for more complete information on the reference sources noted here.)

Conducting a Search

English lexicographer and critic Samuel Johnson said: "Knowledge is of two kinds. We know a subject ourselves, or we know where we can find information upon it." To paraphrase Johnson a bit: The next best thing to *having knowledge* is *knowing where to acquire knowledge*.

There are several reasons for conducting a literature search:

- To find some sources or experts to authenticate your material
- To learn from the experts in your profession
- To find new ideas or new slants for your topics
- To take advantage of the enormous investment made in previous research

A huge amount of information is available in those libraries of literature. All it takes is an investment in time and effort and some direction to follow to locate the proper sources for searching.

To conduct a literature search, follow the step-by-step research procedure outlined in Figure 7-1.

The Big Picture

Your first step should be to those founts of knowledge, the libraries: your own personal library as a starter, then your company library, and finally a university, college, or good-sized public library. If you have trouble locating the right library, the *American Library Directory* (ALD),

Figure 7-1. Literature search procedure.

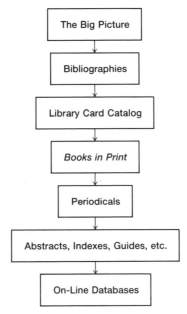

published by R. R. Bowker Co., lists over 35,000 U.S. and Canadian libraries of all kinds. Arranged alphabetically by state and province, it summarizes each library's holdings. Another source is the *Directory of Special Libraries and Information Centers,* published by Gale Research, which lists over 14,000 special libraries and information centers in the United States and Canada and includes an extensive subject index. Libraries established to give the public access to federal government publications are listed in *Federal Government Document Depository Libraries.*

The library you select may not have available on its shelves all the documents you're seeking, but it probably has most of the basic reference books, abstracts, and indexes you'll need. If it doesn't have on hand the specific book, periodical, or report you need, you can probably obtain it through our interlibrary loan.

To obtain the big picture, first review general authoritative write-ups such as you'll find in good encyclopedias (the *Americana* and *Britannica* are especially strong in business, science, and government) or a special subject encyclopedia (*Encyclopedia of Economics, The Encyclopedia of Banking and Finance,* and *McGraw-Hill Encyclopedia of Science and Technology,* for example). These general references usually provide a good broad treatment, a general background, and an introduction to the language of your topic, which gives you more subtopics to explore. For more specific information, review the reference sources usually listed at the end of the write-up; typically they are authoritative, well-established sources. Check them for more in-depth information on your topic. For more help, *A Business Information Guidebook* by Oscar Figueroa and Charles Winkler (New York: AMACOM, 1980) can help you locate material.

Bibliographies

Next check the bibliographies, selective lists of books or articles by a specific author or on a particular subject. Bibliographies are available for most branches of business, and books have a bibliography at the end of the text.

To locate a bibliography on your topic, check your library, the *Subject Guide to Books in Print,* and a bibliography of bibliographies.

Library Card Catalog

Next check the card catalog, which indexes all the holdings of the library you're using. You can search for your topic by subject, author, or title. When you locate something of interest, write down the full call number, the title, and the author of the book or periodical on your index card notes. This information helps you locate the specific book and gives you a general location to browse through on the nearby shelves for related books on the same subject of interest. And if the book is not on the shelf, the librarian will need this information to reserve it for you.

Libraries are gradually shifting over to computerized card catalogs. This computerization of the library's holdings offers a number of excellent features not available in a manual card system. You can:

- Find material more quickly.
- Search by various combinations of author, title, subject, and call number
- Search when you know only part of a title, name, subject, or call number.
- Combine a search for an author with a key word in a title.
- Determine if the book is checked out, and if so, when it is due back.

Books in Print

Books in Print, published by R. R. Bowker, lists books still in print and available from American publishers. Separate sets of volumes are arranged by title, author, and subject. *Paperbound Books in Print* (R. R. Bowker) lists by author, title, and subject in-print paperbacks, mostly by U.S. publishers.

Another excellent source is the *United States Catalog,* which is continually updated by the *Cumulative Book Index.* Published by H. W. Wilson, they list all books published since January 1, 1928.

Periodicals

For up-to-date information, periodical research is a necessity. One of the most popular reference sources is the *Reader's Guide to Periodical Literature.* It contains a subject and author index and covers some of the more popular, general-interest American periodicals that have been published since 1900. It is severely limited in scope, however, since it covers fewer than two hundred of the thousands of periodicals published.

Some periodical indexes have been computerized and are now available in many libraries. These computerized indexes have a much larger scope than *Reader's Guide,* are up to date and easy to use, and generally have abstracts that you can print out for reference. One of the most commonly used in libraries is the Information Access Corporation's *Info Trac.* These types of indexes are continually expanding and will soon be the principal source for periodical research.

Abstracts, Indexes and Guides

A wide variety of abstracts, indexes, guides, directories, and similar material is available for all business subjects. Some representative references for business are listed in Appendix A.

On-Line Databases

A sage once said: "The book you desperately need from the library is always checked out."

A database is an organized collection of information that a computer can search as a unit. It can be a catalog of a manufacturer's products, a library of books or a variety of periodicals, or a computer-readable version of a complete set of encyclopedias. It can include virtually any information that can be converted to digital form and stored for retrieval by a computer. Many databases are collections of abstracts and bibliographies from periodicals. Some databases are specific abstracts collected by specialty organizations. The variety, depth, and diversity of available databases is astonishing.

Databases are sold to or generated by on-line vendors, who, in turn, sell access time. Many individuals can interactively search the databases at the same time. The computer, modem, and telephone provide this access.

Databases provide a number of advantages for those searching for information for a manuscript:

- They help you quickly locate the specific information you need, and you can obtain a printout.
- They are much larger than public and private libraries.
- They can be accessed from virtually any place that has a telephone. No longer do you have to waste time commuting and fighting traffic and parking problems.
- They can be searched by author, title, and subject or combinations of these.
- The information is up to date.
- Specialized databases exist for virtually every profession.
- Information is available when you want it. You need not worry that the book or periodical you need to consult is checked out.
- The information is comprehensive, and you can research to any depth you need.

Needed Equipment

To go on-line, you need a personal computer, a modem, a communications software program, a printer, and a telephone. The basic hookup required is shown in Figure 7-2.

Personal computer. Some vendors' on-line systems function only with major PC brands. Check with the vendors you want to search to determine which computer protocols they accept.

Modem. A modem must be added to most computers. Two basic types of modems are in current use: *circuit board,* which conveniently fits inside a computer, and *stand-alone,* housed in a separate chassis

Figure 7-2. Basic on-line setup.

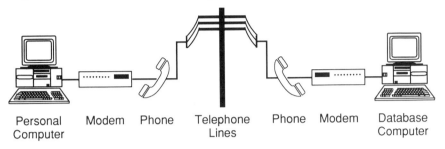

| Personal | Modem | Phone | Telephone | Phone | Modem | Database |
| Computer | | | Lines | | | Computer |

connected to a computer by a cable. The two types have virtually the same capabilities. The circuit board modem does use some power from the computer, and it cannot be easily transported to work on a different computer. The stand-alone modem, typically more costly than the circuit board, has the advantage that it can be moved easily from one computer to another, but mounting and hooking it up can be inconvenient. The stand-alone has light-emitting diodes that help you check on the progress of your query. Stand-alones usually cost more than internal modems.

Regardless of the type you choose, make sure your modem is Hayes compatible, the de facto standard for modems. Fortunately, most modems are compatible with the Hayes command set.

Common speeds are 300, 1200, and 2400 bits per second, with 4800 and 9600 gaining in popularity and 19,200 not far behind. Faster speeds cost more, but even if 9600 costs twice as much as 2400, you receive data at four times the speed. When you choose a modem, make sure it can work at all the common speeds so that you can choose the speed that satisfies your requirements and those of the varied vendors. A speaker on the modem card is also desirable so you can receive audio feedback on the progress of your call.

Software. Software tells your computer and modem what to do. A wide variety of telecom programs is available, ranging in cost from free to a couple of hundred dollars. The following features are desirable in a telecom program:

- *Auto dial,* the ability to dial a number or series of numbers that your computer has previously stored in its memory rather than having to dial the number manually.
- *Auto redial,* the ability to redial a number automatically after a specified waiting period if the line is busy.

- Full duplex (simultaneous two-way transmission) and half-duplex (one-way-at-a-time transmission) capability.
- *Automated sign-on,* which sends the vendor number, your account number, and password to the data bank automatically.
- *Break key,* which halts communication and waits for another command—a useful capability when you discover that you've asked for the wrong information.
- *Data capture,* the ability to record on disk the information sent by the database so you can review it at your leisure.
- *Printout,* the ability to print out information as you receive it.
- *Text file transmission,* the ability to input your message off-line and then go on-line to send your message to the database.
- A *minimum word processing program for composing messages.*

Types of Databases

Three basic types of databases are available from vendors: (1) full text, which provides the entire text of a manuscript to read, (2) bibliographic, which provides bibliographic references and summaries of printed publications. This second type is more numerous than the full text and sometimes has abstracts of information, and (3) factual, which provides information like stock quotes and statistical data.

Some databases are general purpose and cover a wide swath of subjects; others concentrate on specific fields. A large variety of business databases are available. Appendix B lists some of the major ones.

When you deal with databases, you can usually obtain a full-text version of the information you're looking for as a printout at your terminal, or the vendor will send you a photocopy by mail for a nominal charge.

On-Line Costs

The cost of using an on-line system can range from about $3 to more than $200 per hour. In addition, most vendors have a one-time sign-up fee. Check with the vendors to determine individual requirements.

When you're learning how to search an on-line system, use the lower and less expensive rate. After you've acquired some skill, switch to the higher rates. If your budget is limited, there are some excellent after-hours databases to use; the Knowledge Index in the DIALOG system, GEnie, and BRS After Dark have discount rates and excellent varieties of databases.

Searching Once You're On Line

Begin your search with one or more key words, but be careful that the words are not too broad in scope or you'll receive too many "hits" (that is, the number of possible bibliographic references for the key word you have chosen). If this number is too large—say, you come up with 100 when all you anticipated was 10—narrow your search parameters with carefully chosen limiting words and syntax.

The key to an efficient search strategy is to plan in detail what you are going to do *before* you go on-line. Here's a general plan to follow:

1. Write down what you're going to research, and be specific, for example, "Locate a computer drawing program for the IBM XT."
2. From this statement, choose the main concepts or key words to use in your search—for this example, "drawing, graphic." Don't use a common term such as "draw," or you'll be overwhelmed with hits.
3. Limit the key words by restricters to minimize the number of hits. Some restricters are publication title, article type, author, date of publication or range of dates, or Boolean combinations of words, such as "Drawing AND IBM XT."
4. Study the databases the vendor has available, and select the one or two that are the most likely to meet your requirements *before* you go on line.
5. Have your password and account number on hand *before* you go on line.

Once you've located your reference, some vendors will display the abstract on your screen; others permit displaying the entire manuscript; and some vendors will let you download the entire manuscript to your computer.

On-Line Vendors

A number of on-line vendor services are described in Appendix B. Telephone numbers and addresses do change, so if you are unable to obtain a response, dial the 800 line directory assistance service: 800-555-1212. For a more thorough and up-to-date coverage of on-line vendors, consult the following references:

- *Computer Readable Databases.* By Martha Williams. Chicago: American Library Association (latest edition)

- *Database Directory 1984/85–.* White Plains, N.Y.: Knowledge Industries (annual)
- *Datapro Directory of Online Services.* Delran, N.J.: Datapro Research Corp. (latest edition)
- *Directory of Online Databases.* Santa Monica: Cuadra Associates. (quarterly)

When you are considering a vendor, obtain answers to these questions before making your decision:

- Does the system have abstracts, bibliographies, or full text?
- What does the service charge? Are there extra charges for 1200, 2400, and higher bits per second?
- Is hard copy available?
- Is the system coverage comprehensive and up to date?
- Can you search on a time basis (e.g., 1985–1987)?
- Can you use Boolean logic in a search to minimize your hits?
- Does the vendor have local telephone access?

It is estimated that less than 2 percent of the information humanity has generated has been coded and stored in any kind of computer format, so we are seeing only a small part of what lies ahead in the burgeoning profession of information retrieval.

Taking Notes

Record your research notes on index cards. One side is normally lined, and the other is blank. They're stiff and easy to manipulate. Choose a size that's big enough to contain your notes, and stick with that size. The 3- by 5-inch size is most commonly used, unless you take extensive notes.

Follow some general guidelines when you take notes:

1. Write your notes on either the ruled or unruled side of the cards. (I prefer using the unruled side for my notes since I occasionally incorporate a simple figure or illustration along with my notes.) Whichever you choose, be consistent.

2. Put only one idea on a card so that later you can organize them into modules and submodules using the Precedent Sort. An idea or topic may be defined as any small amount of information that will not

have to be broken up so that the parts can be placed at separate points in your outline. At the top of each card put a title, or topic, or subject, or heading or whatever other reference you'll need for reviewing the cards later.

3. Use the opposite side of the card to record bibliographic information. If the note is your own idea, record this fact. When you've accumulated a lot of notes, you may have difficulty later remembering which ideas are yours and which came from other sources.

4. Take many more notes than you need to save yourself a trip back to the library. Later you can prune them down to the essentials.

5. Be careful of using too much shorthand; you may forget what you meant.

6. On each card, write the following information as a minimum: the book or periodical reference, the topic or subtopic title (in the upper left-hand corner for a quick reference), and your notes.

7. Read through your references carefully to make sure you understand them. Then digest the content and write what you've read *in your own words*. Note key ideas, key words, and key phrases.

When you do your research, you'll be taking three types of notes: quotations, paraphrasing, and personal comments. Copy verbatim only if your reference has said something unique, colorful, descriptive, or forceful. You'll find that 90 percent of the time when you take notes, you will be paraphrasing the information. Paraphrasing increases your understanding of the information, suits your purposes better than the quotation, and is usually shorter than the original.

Reviewing Books Quickly

You're not going to have time to review completely all the books you'd like to research, so here are some shortcuts that will give you enough information for your topic:

1. *Skim the book.* Read the chapter titles and the boldfaced headings, and look at the illustrations for a quick summary of the book's contents.
2. *Read the title page.* Note the author, his or her qualifications, and the publication date to see how recent the book is. Also note the publisher. The book is more likely to be an authoritative reference if the publisher specializes in that type of book.

3. *Read the foreword, preface, or introduction.* They state the purpose and intent of the book.
4. *Review the Contents.*
5. *Read the opening paragraphs of each chapter.*
6. *Check the index for topics of interest* and see how many pages are devoted to these topics. If you find some topics that pique your interest, look them up, skim them, and make notes of topics that you feel you can use.
7. *Check the bibliography.* It will reveal the author's sources and whether he or she is using up-to-date information.

8

Top-Down Planning Subroutine

> Write the way an architect builds, who first drafts his
> plan and designs every detail.
>
> —Arthur Schopenhauer

Although different formats are required for specific business documents, the basic methods of designing and writing them are similar.
This chapter develops a universal procedure for designing a document,
and the next one develops a universal procedure for writing a manuscript. These procedures can be used for articles, reports, manuals,
specifications, proposals, and books.

The chapters in Part II will show how these universal procedures
can be used to design and write each of these special formats.

Why Write It Down?

Without a written document, any work accomplished or proposed remains in the heads of the people involved, and we all know how fragile memory is. When the work is written down, the results, objectives,
procedures, conclusions, and recommendations can be simultaneously
disseminated for information, action, review, and evaluation by peers,
management, and other business professionals working in similar fields.
And it becomes an archival document, one that can be referred to long

after the people who worked on it are gone or are busy on other projects.

In many companies (Bell Telephone Labs is a prime example), the only product that is output by the company is the paper (or computer disks) the reports are written on. Documentation is as much a key part of a company's business as the products they produce, the people they employ, and the buildings they occupy.

Using Top-Down Design for Writing

Most creations are designed from the top down. When you design a house, you don't begin with boards and nails; you first envision the overall look of the house—how large it will be and the shape, number, and size of the rooms. You then step down in successive levels of detail. At each level, you design smaller and smaller components of the house: kitchen, cabinets, trusses, closets . . . until you reach the wood and the nails, the basic components of a house.

Good writing also must be designed from the top down. A writer who begins by writing a paragraph or module of a manuscript before an overall design or outline has been created has entered a maze. Without a well-defined path to follow, he or she cannot create a logical progression of numerous topics, compose a complete manuscript, or write a coherent document that can be read and easily understood.

All manuscripts consist of the following components arranged in a specific hierarchy:

Each level of writing can be composed of one or more of its lower subdivisions. For example, an article is a manuscript with only one chapter; a book is a manuscript that is composed of several chapters. Some chapters may consist of only one module; some can have many modules. Some modules may contain only one submodule; other modules can contain many submodules. Some paragraphs will contain only a single sentence; other paragraphs can contain many sentences.

The Universal Subroutine for Top-Down Design

The universal, step-by-step subroutine for top-down design of any component part of a manuscript (a chapter, a module, or a submodule) is outlined in Figure 8-1. This basic subroutine can be used over and over to design any of the subcomponents.

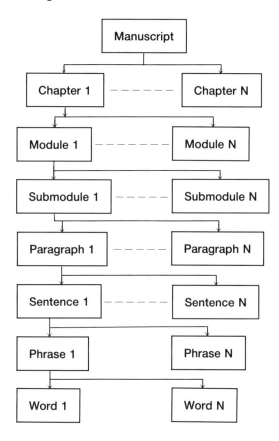

Selecting the Component Topic

Your first component topic will be your title, theme, or purpose or some combination of these that you will use for the design of your individual chapters.* Then select one chapter and design the modules for it, adding this new information to update your outline.

Once the chapter topics are designed, you can design the individual modules for all the other chapters or step down one level in that chapter and design all the modules and submodules in it, again updating your outline. When you complete the modules for one chapter,

*To keep terminology consistent, I'll refer to chapters in a book. This material applies equally to modules in a smaller document, such as a report or article.

Figure 8-1.   Universal design subroutine.

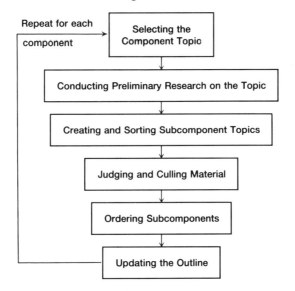

switch to another chapter and design the modules and submodules for it, again updating the outline.

This modular procedure provides you the freedom to design your manuscript in any order and still achieve the completeness, the logical progression of ideas, and the excellent readability that must be a part of every manuscript.

Conducting Preliminary Research on the Topic

Once the component topic is selected, the next step is to conduct research. Two levels of research are used for writing: preliminary and in-depth.

During the design phase, you need to conduct adequate preliminary research to define your manuscript down to the module and submodule levels. Later, during the writing phase, you perform a more in-depth level of research, accumulating enough information to fill in the details of the modules and submodules. Preliminary research will be addressed in this chapter and in-depth research in the next.

Preliminary research, also called quick research, is conducted to obtain enough information to design all the way down to the headings and basic content of modules and submodules. It is a surface type of investigation where you obtain information from general and special subject encyclopedias, general reference books, abstracts, and directories.

When you conduct preliminary research, you don't need to read all the reference books from cover to cover. You can obtain the essence of each book by reviewing the contents page, glancing through the index, reading the preface and the introduction, reviewing the subheads in each chapter, reading the first sentences in some key paragraphs, and seeing how much emphasis the author gave to each of these topics. Make appropriate notes using the techniques described in Chapter 7 as you conduct this preliminary research.

You an also conduct a brief session with an on-line data bank or do some brainstorming, a process where you think creatively and uncritically about a topic without being concerned about the organization, relevance, or importance of your thoughts. It is an idea-generating process where you create without pausing to judge the material, because judging kills the creative cycle.

How to Brainstorm

1. Find a quiet place and get a stack of 3- by 5-inch cards and a pen and relax. If you prefer to brainstorm on your word processor, pull up a comfortable chair and rest your hands on the keyboard, poised to create some inventive ideas.
2. Write down on the card (or type and display on the screen) the module topic you want to expand. As you look at those first words, other thoughts will begin to pop into your mind. Quickly write these thoughts down, one idea or thought per card (or a new line on the word processor for each idea or thought).
3. Write down all questions, statements, thoughts, or ideas you have. *Do not stop to judge them. Write everything down.*

   Ideas are nourished by other ideas. A huge quantity of ideas is needed. You may have sixty-four bad ideas and only one good idea. But that good idea may never have been born unless it was able to feed on the other sixty-three.

   Write down all the ideas that occur to you, even if they may belong in another module, even if they might be duplicates. You can sort them out later.
4. If you get stuck, try using these triggers: What? Why? Where? Who? When? How? Frame these into mind-triggering questions to ask yourself—for example:

- What aspects of my subject should I cover?
- Why is this subject important to my reader?
- Where is my subject used?
- Who has written about my subject?
- When was my subject originated?
- How should I begin my research?
- How many topics should I cover?
- Can my topic be reversed or turned upside down or sideways?

Brainstorming is not a five-minute task; it might take an hour or two, or even longer, depending on the material. As an example, I invested a little over two hours brainstorming this brainstorming module.

When you find that your creative juices have run dry, take a break and do something else. Later, continue where you left off. It's likely that your subconscious mind worked when you were relaxing and created some new ideas.

Creating and Sorting Subcomponent Topics

To create chapter divisions and titles, expand on your purpose, premise, or theme. For this important step, conduct enough preliminary research and/or do more creative brainstorming to expand your manuscript idea in sufficient detail to enable you to divide your topic into a number of parts. You will also need to generate a purpose, premise, or theme, along with a title, or a combination of them for each individual chapter. Keep in mind that when you divide the subject of your manuscript into chapters, the subject matter should be divided into parts of approximately equal size and of equal importance.

Conduct brainstorming and preliminary research for the entire manuscript over a period of time—from a few hours to days or even weeks. Make notes on 3- by 5-inch cards and accumulate them during multiple and varied brainstorming and research sessions. Don't worry about whether the notes are relevant, duplicate, expressed in proper grammar, or earth shaking. Just write down all of your thoughts and research notes on a topic without judging them. Finally you will decide you are saturated on a topic or feel that you have enough information to begin your sort.

Find a large, flat surface (perhaps a floor or a big table) and sit down with your deck of cards. The cards are not in any particular order, so simply begin with the top card and lay it down, face up, on the surface to begin the first column. Look at the second card and see if it is associated with the first card in one of three ways:

1. *Is it a similar topic? Similarity* means that the topics are alike or resemble each other but are not exactly the same (e.g., apples and pears are similar in that both are fruits, but they are not exactly the same).
2. *Is it a contiguous topic? Contiguous* means the topics are neighbors, joined, close together, or adjoining (e.g., the tackle and guard on a football team have adjoining positions on the line).
3. *Is it a contrasting topic? Contrasting* means that one topic is the opposite of another topic (e.g., love and hate are contrasting).

These are important subjective judgments that shouldn't be accomplished without considerable pondering. Take your time in this crucial part of the sorting process.

If the topic of the second card is related to the first card by one of these three categories, place it in the same column, below the first card. If it is not related, place it in a row horizontal to the first to begin a second column. Again, don't be too concerned about getting everything perfect the first time. You can iterate later and move the cards around when you see how the outline is shaping up.

Pick up the third card and make the same comparison. If it passes one of the three tests and is related to the first and/or second card, place the third card in the appropriate column. If it does not pass one of the three association tests, start another column with the third card.

Continue through the deck until you have placed all the cards down and lined them up in the various columns. You should now have somewhere between five and twenty or more columns of cards, where each column contains the cards describing the basic content of a chapter or a module.

Now, with all the cards sorted into columns, you have a rough outline of some of the topics your manuscript will cover. The topics are not organized yet, and there may be some duplications. Review the material to locate any duplications, and eliminate or combine them onto a single card. You may also have some second thoughts about which column the various cards belong in, so review them carefully again to see how they fit.

Judging and Culling Material

You were initially encouraged to accumulate much more material than you would be able to use for your topics and to do this without judgment. Now it's time to judge.

As you review your note cards, ask these questions of each card:

- Is it a duplicate? If so, discard it.
- Does it belong in this column? If not, set it aside.
- Is it relevant? If not, discard it.
- Should it be combined with others? If so, do it.

Don't judge too harshly at this point; you'll have ample opportunity later to cull your material further. Just separate the obvious misfits. If you have doubts about whether a specific topic should be used, leave it in; you may find a home for it later. It is better to err on the side of having too many cards.

Ordering Subcomponents

Once you are fairly well satisfied that your cards have been sorted properly, you are ready to begin ordering:

1. Take one column (one stack of cards) at a time and conduct a Precedent Sort to organize the cards for each individual column.
2. Review each column, and create a title or note that describes its contents. This may be a tentative title for a chapter or a short description of the contents of the column.
3. Write that title or note on a new card, stack the cards from that column in order, and place the title card on top. You now have a stack of cards for a chapter and a title or summary card on top that states the topic that chapter or module will cover. Place a rubber band around the column deck of cards to keep the column in order.
4. Repeat this procedure for each of the other columns. You will end up with somewhere between five and twenty or more stacks of cards, each with a title or note card on top. Each stack of cards forms the basis for a chapter or a module.
5. Use the Precedent Sort to organize all the individual stacks into the desired sequence. Then go through each stack, one at a time and organize them.

You now have the basis for an outline that has been designed from the top down.

Updating the Outline

Input all the organized information from the cards into your word processor, and print it out for review. Carefully review this rough outline to see if any topics are missing, which topics should be combined, or which topics should be divided up or moved.

Remember that top-down design is a continual iterative process. A manuscript doesn't grow in a straight line from the kernel of an idea to an accomplished fact. There are many detours and much retracing of circuitous paths on the way.

Another possible method you might consider for breaking the topic of your manuscript up into chapters (or modules) is assuming that you're going to teach a course covering the entire topic of your manuscript. Divide your subject into ten to twelve lectures (four to eight modules for a short seminar) and decide what you would cover in each of the lectures to teach your topics to a diverse group.

Repeating the Subroutine

Use this same, basic subroutine repeatedly to create a complete outline covering all the other components. For a book, repeat the procedure down to the module and possibly the submodule level. For an article or a short report, perform the subroutine repeatedly down to the module, submodule, and even to the note level below the submodule.

You are now ready to begin writing.

9

Bottom-Up Writing Subroutine

Learning without thought is labor lost; thought without labor is perilous.

—Confucias

When a manuscript is designed down to the smallest component (the submodule), the procedure for writing the individual submodules that comprise the manuscript can begin, using the detailed outline created during the top-down design phase.

The Universal Subroutine for Writing

The subroutine for bottom-up writing of each module is outlined in Figure 9-1.

Selecting the Module Topic From the Outline

To begin, select a module topic from the detailed outline you have created. Choose a chapter that you think will be the easiest to conduct in-depth research on and/or to write, or the topic that you have the most information about. It's not important whether the module is at the beginning, the middle, or the end.

Figure 9-1. Bottom-up writing subroutine.

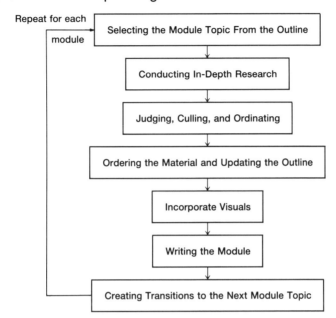

Conducting In-Depth Research

The following suggestions will help you conduct in-depth research on specific topics:

1. *Know how to get help and whom to ask.* There are numerous sources of free information. Many people are eager to help writers. Librarians particularly are well trained in their field and can help you locate virtually anything that exists in their libraries, as well as in other resources.

2. *Do your own research.* Researching is a personal matter. You may not even know precisely what you're looking for when you begin, but as you search, one fact will lead to another and another until, with persistence, you'll find more than enough information for your manuscript.

3. *Check both old and recent periodicals.* More and more indexes and abstracts are being automated, so it's becoming easier and quicker to search for and to locate specific periodical information. Learn how to use these computer-driven tools. If you are searching for a particular

key word and can't locate what you want, try using synonyms, variations, or combinations of the key words.

4. *Review more than one reference book on the same subject.* Authors have different slants, different backgrounds, and different sources and will often cover very different aspects of your topic.

5. *Use on-line databases,* an increasingly authoritative, in-depth source of information. You can obtain information from them relatively quickly and inexpensively if you search efficiently.

6. *Write down not only the sources that gave you information but also the ones that did not* so you won't waste time when you return to continue your research. Also note the library or other source where you found the information so that if you have to go back and verify something, your source will be easy to relocate.

Judging, Culling, and Ordinating

When you were working on your design, you were encouraged to let your creativity flow unfettered, unfenced, and unbiased. Then you conducted research to verify facts, expand your material, answer questions, and make notes without questioning the worth of your information. Now it's time to do that judging.

To judge the notes that you have accumulated so far, use a large, clutter-free, flat surface such as a large table or a floor. You are now ready to begin:

1. Lay all cards for one chapter on this flat surface, face up, and aligned in one or more vertical columns. This order lets you view all of them, quickly compare the topics, and check for relevance to the topic of the specific chapter. To one side, place the top card with the chapter title or summary on it.

2. Review all the cards and eliminate any that are duplicated. If the information on some cards overlaps, combine the material on one card and discard the surplus one or staple the two together.

3. Go through each card one at a time and for each determine if the material it contains is important enough and relevant to be included in the chapter. If not, discard it. You may have to go through your cards a number of times to make these decisions since you will be dealing with relative levels of importance that may not become apparent until you've reviewed all the material for a chapter thoroughly. If you are not certain of applicability, leave the card in. Err on the side of having too much information rather than too little. If you decide that

the information on the card belongs in another chapter, set the card aside, mark the correct chapter number on it, and save it until you work with that chapter.

Ordination is the process of ranking the topics by determining whether each note is important enough to be a chapter, a module, or a submodule and dividing the material into these three categories.

This is one of the most important of all the steps since it determines how much text and how much emphasis you're going to assign to each topic and which topics are going to be included. This need only be a tentative decision since you can iterate and rearrange the cards as many times as required to achieve the desired organization. It's much easier to review and rearrange a nearly correct outline than it is to review and rearrange a mass of random topics.

When you make this tentative decision about each card, write an *s* on top of the card if you decide the topic is important enough to be a submodule, an *m* if you decide it is worthy of being a module heading, and a *c* if it is important enough to warrant devoting an entire chapter to it.

When you've finished with all the cards, set any new chapter cards aside and line up the module (or submodule) cards for the chapter or module you're working on across your surface.

Go through the cards that have been designated as suitable for being a submodule and sort these out under the appropriate module using the three association tests:

1. Is it a similar topic?
2. Is it a contiguous topic?
3. Is it a contrasting topic?

Create one or more modules for any submodule that does not belong in one of the existing modules, and yet still is important to the chapter.

Now you should have all of the material for a chapter or module sorted out (Figure 9-2).

Ordering the Material and Updating the Outline

For each module, order the material using the Precedent Sort. If you discover that some topics are not ordinated properly, make any necessary corrections. Once you have all the modules for a chapter organized, you have the basic outline for that chapter.

Be sure to update your outline when you have finished sorting

Figure 9-2. Sorted-out modules.

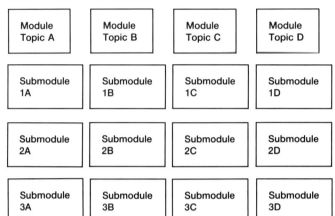

and ordering the information. Input the outline for each chapter into your word processor (or type it up) as soon as you complete the Precedent Sort for the chapter or module. Then review a printout of the outline to make sure it flows well from topic to topic. As you review, you'll probably see some duplication and find some topics that are missing. Revise the outline as necessary, and conduct any additional research you need to resolve inconsistencies or fill in gaps.

Incorporate Visuals

When your outline is complete and your material has been judged and culled, the next step is to add visuals. Some of your modules may not require visuals. If they don't, move on to the next step.

You may have created or sketched out some visuals to enhance your text when you were researching or outlining it, so now is the time to add your visuals. Chapter 5 provided a thorough discussion of which types of visuals to use. Visuals make most complex concepts easier to understand. They enhance an article since every reader sees the same picture. Properly used, visuals save you considerable text. Visuals must be added at this stage of composition so that they form an integral part of the text, instead of being tacked on as afterthoughts.

Writing the Module

As you write the text for the module you've selected, you'll quickly see the value of an outline. A thorough, detailed outline shows that most of your research and creative thinking about the subject has already been accomplished. Most of your information has been researched, collected, interpreted, and interrelated. Writing then becomes primarily a matter of developing your ideas with explanations, discussions, analogies, and examples and of tying them together with the necessary transitions.

With your outline completed and your visuals roughed out, you're ready to write a rough draft. Don't be overanxious about the mechanics of writing. Be more concerned with the content. Concentrate on getting the information down in the proper order.

When you begin writing, you'll discover that a significant advantage of using an outline is that you will be writing about and concentrating on only one module at a time. You can mentally set aside all the other modules for the moment and focus your total faculties on the single module in front of you.

Before you begin to write, remember that you're writing for a specific audience. Keep in mind that your readers do not have much time. They are impatient and anxious for you to get to the point. Reading your prose should require a minimum of their time and effort.

Your readers may have widely varying backgrounds of experience and education. So pause a moment and consider them. Are they:

- From small or large businesses?
- From your profession or from a wide variety of different professions?
- Familiar with the background subject of your manuscript?
- Busy, with little time to read long manuscripts?
- Of varying backgrounds—some technical, some business, some managerial?

Remember that your readers will not be forced to read your work. It's up to you to organize and write it so it's interesting enough to be read.

When you write about something you've been deeply immersed in for so long, you will be tempted to include every pertinent detail. But don't assume your readers will be interested in all these details. They need only enough information to answer the questions, "What is this all about?" "Why should I read this?" Readers will read for the contents, not for the joy of reading your prose.

Follow the steps outlined here in writing the body of your manuscript. It's a proven formula that will help you create a well-written manuscript with a minimum of effort.

1. *Get ready to write.* Find a quiet place where you won't be disturbed—a deserted office, the quiet corner of the company library or lunchroom, someone else's office or a conference room, or a quiet room at home—at the time of day when your mental equipment works the best. Review and read and reread all of your index cards for the module you've chosen. This is the single most important step in the preparation of your manuscript, so invest some time in reading, reviewing, questioning, checking, and double-checking your references. You want this information to sink deeply into your mind.

2. *Take a break.* Put your notes aside, and go off for a while and do something totally unrelated to your manuscript. This gestation period is necessary so that the material you just studied can settle deep in your mind and let that marvelous, magical, mental mechanism, your subconscious, go to work on the material and sort, evaluate, add to, classify, organize, and expand it. It's ideal if you can take this time to engage in some physical activity so that you don't even consciously think about your manuscript.

3. *Write as fast as you can.* For this step, take a lesson from the tale of the centipede and the frog.

One day a centipede was proudly displaying his hundred legs while a mischievous four-legged frog watched. The frog asked him, "When you want to get from Here to There, which of your 100 legs do you move first?"

The centipede began to think. First he tried to move one leg, then the other; then he moved another leg, than another. But to his consternation, he found that if he thought about it first, he was unable to move a single leg without stumbling all over himself. The poor centipede never walked again.

The same thing can happen when you write your rough drafts. If you pause to make sure that your sentences are complete and that you use correct punctuation and the proper words, your fingers are going to stumble rather than race over keys. Rough draft writing must be accomplished with your subconscious mind in high gear.

After you've been away from your material for some time, find another quiet place and get your equipment ready. Sit down in front of your word processor, your typewriter, or your dictating machine or get a supply of pencils or pens and lined paper.

Tack your working outline up on the wall and the visuals you plan to use so you can refer to them. *Don't consult your detailed notes under any circumstances at this point!* If you write directly from notes, you'll end up by simply copying the words directly into your text. The unfortunate result will be a compilation of undigested facts. You'll be using the exact words from your notes rather than putting all of the thoughts and ideas into your own words. Instead, put your individual creativity to work and write using only your working outline and visuals to guide the words from your subconscious to the keys.

Start writing with whatever comes into your head, referring to the outline and to the applicable visuals as you work. In this way, you'll be writing a series of short, easily handled paragraphs rather than one long, continuous one. Write or type as fast as you can, using double or triple spacing for later corrections and additions. Don't pay any attention to grammar, spelling, sentence structure, variety, or length; don't stop to make any corrections; and use incomplete sentences if you must. Just record the words and ideas.

Don't let anything sidetrack you in this highly creative process. Get it all down as fast as you can. You'll find that your enthusiasm will grow once you surmount the initial hurdle of starting. You'll be amazed and pleased at how quickly thoughts come to you. Your hands will not be able to keep up with your brain.

As you finish each submodule, cross it off your outline. If you get stuck on a particular submodule, switch to another one. Chances are that you'll soon get unstuck and be able to go back and finish that submodule later.

The subconscious mind is probably one of the most fantastic creations in existence. It makes a super computer look like a wind-up toy. Used and nourished properly, you'll be amazed at how easily you can turn out good writing fast and almost effortlessly with your subconscious running in high gear.

4. *Check against your detailed notes.* Soon after you've finished writing the rough draft of a module, reread your notes to see if you've left anything out. You probably have, so fill in the blanks left open in the first draft. If you're writing by hand or typing and have left out quite a bit and have to add a page between, say, pages 2 and 3, number it 2a. By using individual sheets of paper, you can add, subtract, or reorganize as required. In a word processor you can easily insert information and corrections. If you're dictating, you'll need to have a rough draft typed first so you can mark it up.

5. *Review the rough draft.* Before reviewing the module, pause a few hours or longer to let your writing cool off. "Write in haste, polish at leisure" is good advice. (While you're waiting, you can choose another module and repeat Steps 1–4.)

When you're ready, review your rough draft. Check sentence length, structure, grammar, punctuation, and spelling, and make any needed corrections. If you're working with a word processor, you may prefer to accomplish the process on the video screen by scrolling through the text or reviewing a printout. (I prefer to use a printed copy since I can flip back and forth to double-check other parts of the manuscript.) Write notes to yourself on the screen or on the printed copy about what to do later, but don't interrupt your reading too long during this process. Read the entire draft through at a leisurely pace.

When you come to a sentence you don't understand, make a note to clarify it, but don't stop to correct it. Wait until the next step.

6. *Revise.* Later, take the time to do the detailed rewrite, making necessary additions and corrections. Put the spelling checker and grammar checker to work if you have them. Use the electronic or manual cut-and-paste to restructure your manuscript. Because second and third thoughts are often clearer than first thoughts, revision can often make the difference between an excellent manuscript and a mediocre one. If you're working with a word processor, perform this revision step with a printout of the entire manuscript, since all of your errors will show up better on paper and you can easily jump back and forth to check and verify.

Repeat this procedure for a different module, in the same chapter or in a different one. Check your detailed outline to decide which module you'd like to write next.

Creating Transitions to the Next Module Topic

You should already have completed your paragraph-to-paragraph transitions when you wrote the text. The next level of transition required is from module to module.

Once you have completed all or most of a chapter, check to make sure that the module-to-module transitions are good. These transitions can often be accomplished by the use of a subhead that introduces the next topic. If the change in topics is considerable, write a transitional sentence at the end of one module that introduces the next module and illustrates how the topic of the first module ties directly into the topic of the second one.

Chapter titles provide chapter-to-chapter transitions and are similar to module-to-module transitions, except that a much larger change in subject is permitted from one chapter to the next. Still, chapters must follow the general plan of the book and not deviate from the logical series of topics discussed.

If you're not sure about which transitions to use, make a note to yourself to take care of it later.

Reviewing the Manuscript

Whether you should review and revise your manuscript each time you write a rough draft or, at the other extreme, wait until the entire manuscript is completed depends on the type of material you're dealing with, your schedule, and your personal preferences.

Experiment with various methods to see which suits you best. My only caution to you is not to become too concerned with grammar, construction, or spelling early in your rough drafts.

Beautifying the Body

Now that you have your manuscript drafted, it's time to beautify the body—adding lists, and subheads, for example—to make your manuscript easier to read and to understand. Experts agree that graphic relief creates white space and makes large blocks of text more readable. Just like the green areas in cities, the blank spaces in documents are mentally refreshing and stimulate the reader's attention. I call these graphic reliefs literary cosmetics. Common literary cosmetics are paragraphing, bullets, lists, subheads, and italics.

Paragraphs

Review your material to check on paragraph length. Most should be fewer than ten typewritten lines (about a hundred words). A final typed page should have at least three or four paragraphs.

But don't overdo it. Too many short paragraphs distort the effect you're trying to create: lots of white space, variety, and a break for the reader's eyes.

A reader sees a paragraph as a certain amount of information he or she must gulp down in one mental swallow, so make the swallows short. Short paragraphs throw more light or understanding on your page, making it easier to read. Paragraphs also help your reader group and understand concepts better.

Bullets

Bullets are a device used to highlight information set off from the text to emphasize specific points—for example:

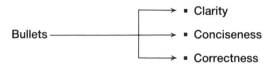

They're another effective way to give the reader's eyes and mind a break. But don't overdo them either.

Lists

Lists enumerate items in a sequence, setting them off as individual, important topics—for example:

1. Grammar
2. Sentence structure
3. Spelling

Lists provide a quick way to summarize points and to emphasize items. They take up more space than sentences, but they highlight the data they present.

Subheads

Subheads—short headlines that summarize and introduce the important facts in the paragraphs that comprise the module—provide effective graphic relief for large masses of text. They provide a visible outline of the manuscript, show the main points you want to emphasize, and highlight the importance of certain material.

Subheads introduce topics and illustrate the order in which they are covered. Readers can obtain a quick summary of a well-written manuscript by reading the headings, noting the order in which they're arranged and the amount of space allocated to each. They can whet a reader's appetite and entice him or her into reading your entire manuscript.

You need about one or two subheads per two typewritten pages of 500 words to allow more space on the page. Subheads should be fewer than five or six words long; two or three words are common.

When your manuscript is published, the headings will probably be set in **boldface** type so they'll stand out even more.

Subheads serve another purpose: They provide a bridge from one module to the next without resorting to such much-abused transitions as "On the other hand" or, worse, "Meanwhile, back at the ranch."

Italics

Italics (or underlining) in the text of a document calls attention to a specific word or phrase you want to emphasize as being important. You're asking your reader to note those words especially.

Remember that business documents are seldom read from beginning to end. People tend to skip around. They'll return later to reread the specific parts they're interested in. The literary cosmetics help readers locate the important parts.

Part II
Modular Writing Applications

10

The Article

An article is a business communication written specifically for publication in a professional periodical or journal. It is not as detailed as a report and can vary in length from about 1,000 to over 4,000 words. About 2,000 to 2,500 words is the average. A double-spaced, printed draft has about 250 words per page, so an article can range in length from 4 to 16 rough-draft pages, not too intimidating a task.

A typical three-column, 8½- by 11-inch page of a professional publication contains about 1,000 words. If you use about two visuals per page, they'll occupy about one-third of the printed page, leaving about 700 words per page. From these figures you can calculate the printed pages your article will fill since many periodicals pay by the printed page.

Why Write an Article?

Writing an article is the easiest and best way for business professionals to become published for the first time. Among the many advantages of writing an article and having your name listed as the author are the following:

- An article may be your only output that will reach upper management. Write well, and you'll be recognized for it.
- You'll promote and help your company's business and improve your chances for advancement. It's a "publish and flourish" situation.
- The person who writes well is looked upon as a leader in his or her profession.

- You'll learn more about any subject when you research, outline, and write about it. Writing is truly a learning experience.
- You're contributing knowledge to your specialty—helping others to learn.
- A list of publications looks impressive on your résumé. In some academic professions, it's a "publish or perish" world.
- You'll earn some money for your efforts.
- You'll earn an inner satisfaction, a pride in what you've accomplished—perhaps the most important reward of all.

Before Writing for Publication

For those of you who are employed by a company and wish to write for publication, check your company policies to see if all your external publications must be approved before submittal. Usually your legal or patent department can advise you on the procedures to follow to obtain company approval. Companies usually insist on approving everything you write for business periodicals and publications to make sure you're not revealing company proprietary information. Your company may also have rules against your working for other companies ·vhile in their employ.

So before you go too far with writing for publication, check your company procedures. I've found that companies are usually very supportive of their employees' publishing articles, as long as the author's company affiliation is added to the write-up. As part of their approval cycle, companies may also insist on reviewing your final manuscript before it is submitted for publication.

Creating the Article

Figure 10-1 diagrams the step-by-step subroutine required to brainstorm, create, research, divide into modules, and write the modules that comprise an article. A module is a portion of an article, usually prefaced by a subhead. Some of these steps have already been examined in Chapters 8 and 9. This chapter focuses on the steps unique to writing articles.

Figure 10-1. Procedure for creating an article.

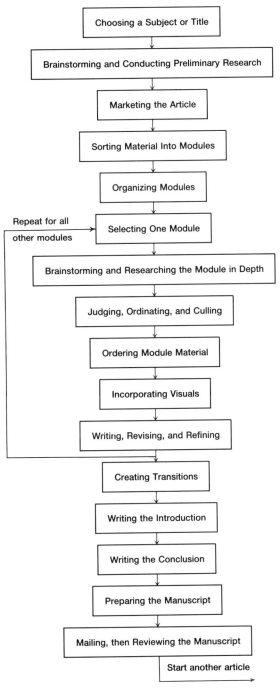

Choosing a Subject or a Title

The most important decision you will make in writing an article is selecting the subject. Choose a good subject, and the research, writing,
and marketing of your masterpiece will be a pleasure. Select a bad subject, and writing it will be drudgery, and publishing it next to impossible.

A good subject for an article should have as many of the following
characteristics as possible. The more it has, the more likely it will be
published.

- *The article benefits readers.* This is the most important requirement.
If it does not benefit readers, it won't be published. Remember that
articles are usually read on an as-time-permits basis, so the subject must
be informative enough for readers to want to spend their time reading it.

- *The subject interests a wide readership.* The audience for an article
includes many nonspecialists. If your subject interests a wide readership, its publication chances are enhanced. Choose a subject that has
wide appeal and broaden its appeal even more by thinking of other
diverse uses or multiple applications for it.

- *The subject is topical.* Because of the constant and rapid explosion
of technologies and changing methods of conducting business, a determined effort is required to keep pace. Short, succinct, informative, and
well-written articles on the latest developments are an excellent way of
learning what is going on in one's profession. Professionals don't have
time to take a sabbatical from work and return to school to catch up,
so they depend on publications to keep themselves up to date. When
you write well of topical matters, you're helping fellow professionals
learn of new developments.

- *The subject is unique.* Uniqueness in a subject can be manifested
in the superlatives of your profession. If your subject covers a product,
procedure, development, or process that is the newest, biggest (or
smallest), fastest, cheapest, or simplest, you have a built-in readership.
If applicable, use the appropriate superlative in your article title.

- *You know something about the subject or can invest enough time to
research it thoroughly.* If it's a subject you know a lot about, you can
write about it with authority, and your readers will respect you for

your knowledge. If it's a subject you know little about, you can research it in depth and become an expert. Even if the subject has been covered many times, adding a new slant or updating the information makes for a readable article. By reviewing the works of others, evaluating them, and contributing some of your own ideas and your unique viewpoint on the subject, you can qualify to be published as an expert.

Although you don't need to be too concerned about creating an exact title for some time, choose a working title right away to help you maintain a focus. As you do research, you'll think of other titles; jot them all down. One idea will lead to another, and eventually you'll come up with an informative, interesting title.

A title should accomplish three main objectives:

1. Catch the reader's eye.
2. Summarize the article.
3. Encourage the reader to keep reading.

Titles cannot be copyrighted, so you can review, revise, and adapt previously used titles for your article.

When you conduct research, review what others have said about your subject or determine the types of articles that appear in the periodicals you want to write for. Make sure your subject hasn't been overdone. As you review this material, note how often certain of these key words appear in the titles:

- *How to*
- *New*
- *Unique*
- *Smallest*
- *Easy*
- *Fastest*

If you can use one of these eye catchers in your title, it will hook the reader into reading on.

A good title is actually a short summary of an article; it describes its contents. It can't be too long—no more than six to eight words. Most titles are sentence fragments. Use the active tense and words that are specific, familiar, common, and short; avoid jargon. Add a subtitle if you need to expand on the title.

Marketing the Article

Choosing a Periodical

You may have certain periodicals in mind you would like to write for, or you may have to do research to determine which publish material on your subject. The key reference books that will help you locate potential publishers to query are listed in Appendix A. Identify at least three possible publishers.

Querying the Editor

One way to market an article is to write it and then send it to a publisher. This method is fraught with uncertainty, however. You may have chosen a subject completely alien to the periodical or one that has been overdone. Or perhaps your length, style, or format may not suit the publisher. Some chain-owned publications are entirely staff written, so you would have no chance of publication with them.

A second way is better: Query the publisher and then, when you get the go-ahead, write the article. If you query first:

- You'll make proper contact with the person who will decide whether to accept your work.
- The editor will tell you if the subject is of interest to the periodical's readers and will advise you about preferred length and format so you can frame your article with this knowledge in mind.
- You'll receive a quick answer (a week or two) to a query; you may have to wait months for a reply to a completed article.

The following guidelines will help you write an effective query:

- Address your letter to a specific editor by name and title. Look up the editor's name on the masthead of the periodical or obtain it from one of the reference books you consulted.
- Get to the point right away! In the first paragraph, hook the editor into reading the rest of your query.
- Be brief. A one-page typed, single-spaced query should be enough, no matter how complex the subject.
- Summarize your article, but provide enough specific information so the editor can make an intelligent decision without being confused about the scope and coverage of the subject.

- Include your proposed title, estimated article length, and the number of illustrations planned.
- Establish your qualifications.
- Inform the editor how long after go-ahead you will deliver the article.
- Request a copy of the periodical's writing guidelines.
- Determine if you should provide a hard and/or soft copy and the preferred format.
- Enclose a self-addressed, stamped envelope (SASE) to make a reply easier and faster.

Figure 10-2 contains a sample query letter.

Figure 10-2. Sample query letter for an article.

February 22, 1992

Mr. Fred Barnes, Editor-in-Chief
Business Today
1030 North Broadway
New York, N.Y. 10020

Greetings Mr. Barnes,

As editor-in-chief, you appreciate how vital proper
business communications are and that business professionals waste too much time writing and reading memos and
letters. In a recent survey of 200 executives of the na-
tion's 1,000 largest corporations, the personnel agency
Accountemps learned that executives waste 32 minutes
every day reading and writing unnecessary memos. I have a
writing formula that will help eliminate much of this
enormous waste of manpower.
    My four part formula is:
              ▪ HEY! ▪ YOU! ▪ SEE? ▪ SO!
HEY! calls the reader's attention to the topic; YOU!
brings the reader into the memo; SEE? is the body of the
memo; SO! is the conclusion, the call for action or reso-
lution.
    I've used and fine-tuned this formula over the past

(continues)

Figure 10-2 (*continued*)

twenty-five years of working as an engineering manager
and writer. I'd like to present my discoveries to your
readers in my article, "Write to the Point." My article
thoroughly illustrates the application of this formula
with examples. It will be about 3,000 words in length and
use four visuals. I can supply my article on hard copy and
on an IBM-compatible 5¼-inch disk (Word Perfect 5.1 or
ASCII) or a Macintosh 3.5-inch disk (WORD 3.0).

I'm a full-time freelance writer with a B.S.E.E., and
have published seven nonfiction books and over thirty
articles in national publications. My latest book, *Writing Better Technical Articles*, was recently published by
McGraw-Hill. I've devoted much of my book and my writing
career to showing how to achieve improved business communications.

Please send me a copy of your writer's guidelines.
May I hear from you soon on this exclusive query? I've enclosed an SASE.

Sincerely,

Harley Bjelland

Harley Bjelland
P.O. Box 687980
Mystic City, Minn. 57684

A Caution

Do not send simultaneous queries to a number of competitive
publishers! You won't save any time by doing this, and you may
end up with two publications that want your article. It's difficult
to retreat gracefully from such a situation—and editors have long
memories. Play it safe and query only one editor at a time.

Within a week or two, you should receive a reply to your query.
This reply can take one of three forms:

1. Your proposal is accepted, and you are invited to write and
   submit a complete article.

2. Your proposal was a little off the mark. The editor offers some suggestions for modifying your outline or your approach before you submit a completed article.
3. Your proposal is rejected. Perhaps your subject wasn't suited to the periodical, or it has been overdone. Or maybe the editor just had a bad day.

Congratulations if you receive either of the first two responses. You're about to write an article and have it published. If your proposal is rejected, review your query letter for improvement, and then quickly address another letter to one of the other publishers you've identified as a possibility, and mail it out right away! There's nothing like the renewed hope of being accepted the next time out to assuage the disappointment of a rejection.

Actually, there is another type of response: The editor replies to your query with, "We'd love to publish your article; however, our editorial policy requires that an author must pay $100 a page for the privilege of being published in our periodical." Simply reply, "No thanks," and send your query to an editor who is buying or who will at least publish it at no charge to you. (Some professional journals operate on a limited budget, and you may not even receive an honorarium for your publication, but the least a publisher can do is publish your writing without charging you.)

You may be able to contact your editor on the telephone and discuss your query, but this is risky. Be well-prepared for such a contact. Have all of your questions and notes on hand when you talk. If you catch the editor at a bad time, he or she may not be receptive to *any* ideas. Having worked as an editor, I know how busy an editor's day can be. Most editors prefer that you write your query, mail it, and give them an opportunity to review it at their leisure and discuss it with their co-workers or staff.

Once you receive a go-ahead for your article, you need to conduct in-depth research for each module, organize your material (creating an outline in the process), and follow the steps for bottom-up writing outlined in Chapter 9.

Writing the Introduction

The introduction is the most important module of the entire article. It must hook the reader into going on, or your article will go unread.

An introduction must live up to its name and introduce the subject to your readers. It must "tell them what you're going to tell them." By the end of the introduction, readers should know what the article is all about, the slant you've taken, and the depth to which the topic will be covered.

Here's an introduction from an article I had published on visual aids:

> **Sooner or later you're going to have to give a talk, perhaps at a program-review meeting or a technical conference, in a discussion on a proposal's technical aspects, or as part of a presentation to management. And, when you do, you'll discover that visual aids, in conjunction with your oral presentation:**
>
> **▪ Provide an outline of your talk for you and your audience to follow.**
> **▪ Help keep the audience's attention.**

Note that the "you" is in the first sentence and that bullets are used to break up the solid look of the first paragraph.

Writing the Conclusion

The conclusion is the second most important module of your article. A satisfying conclusion rewards the readers with the good feeling that they have invested their time wisely in reading the entire article.

The conclusion is a summing up: "Tell them what you told them." It must logically follow from the material leading up to it.

Here's the conclusion from my article on visual aids:

> **Use a lot of visuals the next time you have to give a speech. You'll find that they do much of the talking for you.**

In this short conclusion, "you" appeared three times. And the point of the entire article is neatly encapsulated in the final sentence.

HEY! YOU! SEE? SO!

Whatever happened to the Four Part Formula? Is it also useful for articles? Absolutely!

The title, the subtitle, and the introduction are the HEY! and

YOU! that attract readers' attention and convince them that the information is of interest. The body of the article presents the SEE?—what it's all about. The conclusion section is the so!

You can apply *all* the techniques for organizing and presenting information you've learned in the earlier chapters to writing a business article . . . no matter how complex it is.

Preparing the Manuscript

Figure 10-3 shows the relative attention-getting parts of an article.

Figure 10-3. Attention-getting values of parts of an article.

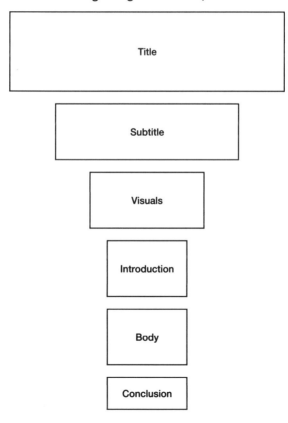

- *Title.* This is the first thing readers will see. Not only do you need a good title, you have to shout it out with a bold headline. Your publisher makes the final decision about graphically displaying the title, but it doesn't hurt to make a suggestion so that your title will have eye-catching appeal—for example:

SPREADSHEETS—DANGEROUS TOOL?

- *Subtitle.* Second in commanding attention, the subtitle should elaborate on your title. Titles are usually limited to a few words since they are in large letters. Subtitles should be in smaller-sized type and can have anywhere from ten to twenty words to expand on the article's contents—for example:

ADDICTED TO THE SPREADSHEET HABIT? WANT TO GO COLD TURKEY?

- *Visuals.* The visuals you use—photographs, drawings, graphs, tables, charts—will be the next hook for your article. They should always appear at least on the first page of your article.
- *Introduction.* This is the final hook that will help your reader decide whether to read the rest of your article. Once the introduction grabs him or her, your reader can't avoid perusing at least part of the body.
- *Conclusion.* You can reword your first paragraph and leave your reader with some satisfactory thought or a call to action. It can recommend a different approach or further investigation, urge acceptance of a new standard method, or in some other way encourage readers to some kind of action. Usually one paragraph is adequate, but use more if you need to.

Mailing, then Reviewing the Manuscript

When you are satisfied you have done the best possible job on your masterpiece, prepare it for mailing.

For the final manuscript, use a new ribbon if you have to, or tune up your laser printer because appearances are important to editors. If you use a dot-matrix printer, use the near-letter-quality mode. A clean, neat, attractive manuscript comes from a person who takes pride in his or her work. Double-space the manuscript.

If your editor requires a soft copy in addition to the hard copy, as more are doing and as more will be doing in the future, include a diskette mailer along with the hard copy. There is no need to include an SASE since it's now the publisher's function to handle the manuscript most of the way through to printing.

If you have photographs or other visuals to mail with your manuscript, protect them by sandwiching them between two sheets of cardboard. Put a big rubber band around the cardboard to keep the filling in the sandwich.

Always send a cover letter with your manuscript to remind the busy editor that he or she has solicited this article so it doesn't end up in an "I'll-get-to-it-when-I-have-time" slush pile. Send everything first class.

You will probably receive a proof copy before publication. Review it carefully, and don't try to rewrite it at this late date. It's already been scheduled and sized for publication, so correct only the typos or other errors you find. Mail it back as soon as you can. Time waits for no late author.

Starting Another Article

Thorwaldsen, the noted Danish sculptor, was once asked by an admirer, "Which do you consider your greatest statue?"

Without hesitation, the famous Dane replied, "My next one."

You should be satisfied with the article you just completed and feel confident that your next one will be your greatest.

It seems as if it takes forever to complete the process from initial concept to publication. Often it can take from six months to a year. So don't sit around waiting for your article to appear; keep yourself busy by researching another article. Once you complete your first article, the second becomes much easier and will be better. With your second done, the third becomes easy. By the time you have your fourth published, you'll start thinking that a dozen or so articles can add up to a book. So why not write a book? Chapter 15 will show you how.

11

The Report

A report is written for the permanent record to document the results of a study, a program, a conference, a trip, or a telephone conference. Often it is the only tangible result of hundreds of hours expended on an investigation of a problem or a study.

A report can be written by a group and addressed to its parent organization or to a client, by an outside consultant for a customer, or by an individual for his or her company management or an outside agency.

The report, the second most common business document (second only to the letter or memo), is one of the most important methods of communicating information. It is vital to the efficient operation of businesses and government. Reports are written not only for archival purposes; they are also written to be read. And if you want your reports to be read, make effective use of some of the techniques that enhance reader interest discussed in Chapter 10.

The Magic Three

No matter what type of format you use for writing your report—a fill-in-the-blanks preprinted form, an electronic form, an essay type, or some other form—the "magic three" should always be a part of every report:

1. Introduction
2. Body
3. Conclusion

Reports can range in length from a short paragraph describing interim activity over a period of a day or a week to a multivolume document describing the results of many individuals completing work on a multimillion dollar project, over a period of a year or more.

A vital point to keep in mind, no matter what type of report you write, is that the first thing your reader wants to know is, "What is this all about?" That important question must be answered right away, and for that reason, a chronological organization should be avoided. Readers don't want a step-by-step account of your project. They want to know what you were supposed to do, what you did, how you did it, and what it proved or disproved. The readers are more interested in where you ended than in where you started.

General Guidelines

The first step in preparing a report is to gather all the available information and list the work to be documented. Like all other business writing, it's important to design in detail what you're going to write rather than to write whatever pops into your head in a random order. An undesigned report is often a rambling, obtuse, confusing document that skips around from one subject to another; few will be inclined to read it. An unread report is a waste of time and effort.

Before you begin, outline your report in a fair amount of detail. Once outlined, writing is much easier; the flow of ideas and conclusions is logical, and you can write modularly. Ease yourself into writing by selecting the portion of the report that is easiest for you to write. Once the first module is completed, writing the other modules, in whatever sequence suits you, is much easier.

A report should be relatively self-sufficient. Your reader should not have to refer to a number of other documents to understand its content. Your report should be thorough, concise, and free of bias.

Know Your Audience

Remember that you're writing for a specific audience. Your readers may be in your company—or they may be all the managers, business professionals, and staff personnel in the world who are interested in the subject you're writing about. It's a good idea to sketch out a distribution list before you write so you'll know how to slant your material, what order to use, what to include, and what to omit.

So pause a moment and consider your audience carefully. Are your readers:

- Your co-workers and management?
- Of similar backgrounds?
- Of varying backgrounds—some business, some technical, some managerial?

Each of your readers will read your report from his or her own viewpoint and with personal interests in mind. If your audience is principally business or management oriented, emphasize the business and managerial aspects of your project. For a technical audience, concentrate on the scientific and engineering portions of your work. If your audience is both business and technical, strike a proper balance that will satisfy both ends of the audience spectrum.

Redundancy

> Tell them what you're going to tell them,
> Tell them,
> Tell them what you told them.

This adage may seem to endorse redundancy—and it should, especially for the longer formats. One important point that applies to most business writing of any length is that a certain degree of redundancy is not only desirable but necessary. Few in your audience will read your entire document. Many will scan it and read only the specific parts or topics of interest to them. It's advisable to repeat certain key phrases, concepts, and so on from time to time not only to reemphasize but also to clarify the ideas.

Be subtle in using redundancy, or rephrase the text so it doesn't sound too much like obvious repetition. Often when you restate your idea at another place in your text, your subconscious will have worked on it, and it will be better stated than the original. Similarly, the reader who reads it stated in two different ways has a better chance of understanding it. Many business concepts are complex, so it helps to restate the same idea in slightly different ways. If you need help in rephrasing, that's what a thesaurus is for. You probably have an electronic thesaurus as part of your word processing program. Use it.

Like most other concepts, however, redundancy can be overdone. Use it judiciously.

For a clear understanding, be sure to define all new terms, abbreviations, acronyms, and symbols the first time they're used in the text. If you're introducing considerable new terminology, repeat all the definitions, abbreviations, acronyms, and symbols in an alphabetically organized glossary.

Formats

Commonly accepted formats are an excellent idea for reports. They help you organize your material, have been proved to work through constant use and revision, jog your memory to make sure you've included all the needed information in the proper order, and make it easier for readers to know where they can locate specific information.

Every report, without exception, should have as a minimum the following features:

- *Date.*
- *Distribution List.* Place it at the start of every report so all addressees will know who the other addressees are. Some reports will have both action addressees (TO:) and information addressees (INFO COPIES TO:).
- *Originator(s).* Display the author(s) of the report and their affiliation(s) prominently near the beginning of the report to inform the reader of the source, orientation, and authority of the information and provide a point of contact if the reader has questions about the report.
- *Subject.* Prepare a short, concise statement of the subject of the report to help readers determine if they should read the entire report, act on it, refer it to someone else for information or action, or discard it.
- *Introduction/Summary.*
- *Body.*
- *Conclusions/Recommendations.*
- *Other Documents.* Some companies or sponsoring agencies may require a letter of transmittal, a letter of authorization, or a similar type of cover letter to be sent with the report.

General Report Format

Most general reports use the following format (although not all modules are needed for every report):

1. Title page
2. Contents, illustrations, tables
3. Abstract (or Summary)
4. Introduction
5. Body
6. Conclusions
7. Recommendations
8. Appendages

The title page, contents, abstract, and introduction are the HEY! and YOU! that attract the reader's attention and convince the reader that the information is of interest. The body presents the SEE?—what it's all about. And the conclusions and recommendations modules are the SO! Thus, you can apply all the techniques for organizing and presenting information you've learned in the earlier chapters to the writing of a general report.

Title Page

Everyone reads the title, the most important phrase of the entire report. It should be fewer than eight to twelve words and be, in effect, a short, well-conceived abstract of the report. The title is usually the first item the reader sees, so it should stand out alone in the center of the title page with a lot of white space around it (Figure 11-1).

Because the title is often used for indexing, filing, and abstracting reports, it should be descriptive enough so readers can understand precisely what is covered in the document. For example, instead of a nondescriptive name, such as "Xyllium Investigations," use a descriptive title, such as "Measurement of Optron Centers in Xyllium-25," so that anyone who looks at only the title can decide if he or she is interested in investing time in reading the report. This is especially important when your document is selected for use by an on-line data bank since the title is the first item the researcher sees.

But be brief. Titles need not be complete sentences; use sentence fragments. Delete redundant words, such as "A Report on . . ." Obviously it's a report. And don't use "An Investigation into the Effects of . . ." Make it "Effects of . . ."

Figure 11-1. Title page for a report.

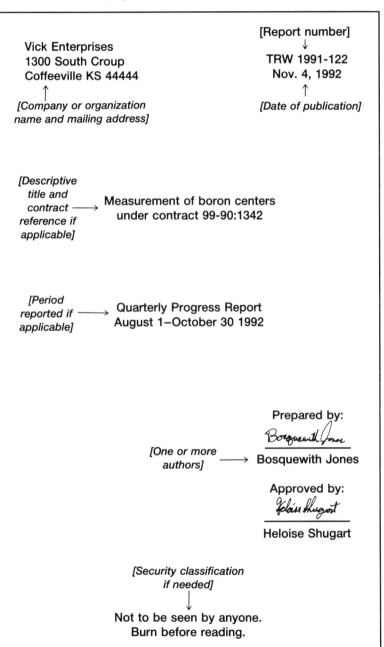

If you're stuck for a title, write down a temporary working title. Often a more appropriate title will come to you when you're working on another module of the report. If you're still in doubt, write down a number of possible titles to trigger your thinking or select the best title in the list you came up with.

Contents

For reports longer than six to ten pages, the contents ("table of contents" is superfluous) should be on a separate page—the second one of the report.

The contents page provides a brief outline of the report, so list all modules, headings, and subheadings, properly indented to show the relative rank and subdivisions of the topics. The contents listing helps readers locate specific topics of interest without having to search through the entire report.

If you number the headings and subheadings, don't use roman numerals! They were all right when Nero was fiddling around but are out of date in our modern, computerized, English-speaking world. The decimal system is universal and easy to understand and use, and the numerals can easily be subdivided, such as 10.24, 11.1, 196.3.2 to indicate levels of headings.

Include an illustrations page (a list of the illustrations) if you have many illustrations and, if needed, a tables page (a list of the tables), following illustrations.

Abstract

The third section contains the most important part of your report: the abstract (or summary). It belongs ahead of the text and on a separate page.

The abstract is a concise summary of the report that will be read by many more people than will read the entire report, so use your best efforts in writing an informative abstract. Most executives and management personnel read abstracts to decide if they should read the report, route it, or skip it. Often the abstract is the only part of the report that upper-level management will read. You may be partially judged by those who will eventually have to approve your raises and promotions by the abstracts you write. Moreover, abstracts are becoming increasingly important as documentation is added to on-line data banks.

One of the biggest daily chores that business professionals have is reading. They must review memos, reports, periodicals, brochures, newsletters, and other material to keep pace with their profession, but they don't have the time to read through all the material they receive, so a concise and well-prepared abstract is essential to help reach the largest audience possible.

An abstract summarizes the topics of the report in enough detail so that the reader can determine whether the subject is of enough interest to read the rest of the report. People with a wide variety of backgrounds will read your abstract, so write it for a broad readership. Avoid jargon, clichés, and highly complex and highly technical terms. Use well-established, commonly understood terminology.

Requirements

The abstract should briefly describe the following:

- Problem or task
- Course of action
- Results
- Conclusions
- Recommendations

It should not list all the trials and tribulations you and your co-workers encountered in struggling from the problem to the solution. Briefly review the main tasks and then list the results, conclusions, and recommendations, without justification. The body of your report will cover the results.

Don't begin the abstract by repeating the title of the report, because these two parts invariably end up together in an on-line data bank. But you can use subheadings and minor graphics to aid in understanding and to save text. Remember that the abstract should not contain information that is not in the body of the report.

Outlining First

Outline the entire report first, and then use the outline to help write your abstract. Again use the pattern of the "magic three:" introduction, body, and conclusion (recommendations).

Some books recommend that you write the abstract last, after you have completed your entire report—but that's backward. You should draft your abstract first, before writing the report. The abstract is supposed to inform the reader what the report is all about. And if you, the writer, don't know what it's all about before you write it, you'd better pause and get your thoughts in order.

Preparing the abstract first has several advantages:

- It helps you organize your report.
- You are forced to get to the point.
- It helps you limit what you want to say without wandering about aimlessly.
- It's a good discipline.

Often when you write the body of a report, you'll add topics that aren't mentioned in your abstract. Make appropriate notes, and when the report is drafted, revise your abstract accordingly. It's much easier to revise a nearly correct abstract at this point than it is to create it totally anew.

A primary rule about an abstract is:

Keep it short!

Even for moderately complex reports, an abstract should be no more than ten to fifteen lines long (100 to 150 words—less than half a page) and no more than about six to eight sentences. At the other extreme, a one- or two-sentence abstract would hardly tell readers what they need to know.

For longer reports (fifty to a hundred pages), an abstract can be up to a page in length. Even a short report (five to ten pages) deserves an abstract because it saves readers' time.

Here's an abstract for this chapter:

Chapter 11 covers reports written to provide a permanent record of activities. General guidelines, along with specific formats and content, are recommended for the following types of reports:

- Project/program
- Study (investigation)
- Activity
- Trip (conference)
- Telephone conference

Major considerations in report writing include: outlining, knowing your audience, including certain basic information, and the moderate use of redundancy. Examples of special formats are given for each type of report listed above.

The abstract contains seventy words; it's about 1½ percent of the length of the body of the chapter, which contains about six thousand words.

Introduction

The introduction introduces the material and orients readers to the report. It should be one to two pages at the most for a lengthy report. Because of the wide variety of backgrounds of the individuals who read it, an introduction should use lay language and refrain from using jargon or complex terms.

The introduction provides the background for the work described in the body and should include as a minimum the subject of the report (the problem), why the work was done (the purpose), the scope of work, the method of attacking the problem, and background.

• *Subject.* The first sentence(s) announces the subject of the report in clear, concise statements. What is this all about?

"This report describes the effects of antiacid medicine on pregnant sheep."

• *Why?* If the readers are interested in the subject of the report, their next question is, Why was the report written? What function does the report serve? Why was the work done?

The purpose of this report is to show that pregnant sheep. . .

• *Scope.* Next, outline the scope of the work—the limits of the subject. The limits could be in the amount of detail included, whether broad or limited. Time and/or budget limitations of the work, the facilities, and other factors that limited the scope should be discussed—for example:

Because of the lengthy gestation period and the availability of only a single, aged ram, the scope of the study was considerably limited.

- *Methodology.* Discuss the methods used in solving the problem. What facilities were used, what equipment? How were the tests or evaluations made? Was it a study, or an experiment, or an evaluation? Was a computer program used? Which one? What were its limitations?

- *Background.* Finally, briefly cover any business, technical, or historical background that is needed to understand the report. Properly done, the background can pique a reader's interest about the contents of the report. But it should be limited to no more than a page or you'll defeat the purposes of an introduction. For a more extensive background or if only a small number of your readers need it, provide an appendix titled "Background" so the material is not in the way of most readers but can be reviewed by those who need it.

The introduction is not a rehash of the abstract; it is a bridge transporting a reader from what he or she knows to a point where he or she has acquired the knowledge needed to understand the text. The starting point for the introduction is, "Where is your reader coming from?"

So, pause a moment and answer the questions about your reader that were listed earlier in this chapter under "Know Your Audience." If your intended audience consists of your co-workers and company management, they need only a short orientation, perhaps explaining the reason for the project, the objectives, the sponsoring organization, the personnel involved, and any references to related or earlier projects.

If you are addressing a wide variety of readers, some inside your company and others outside, with a business or technical background but in a different specialty, the function of an introduction is complicated.

If your readers are of varying backgrounds—some technical, some business, and some staff—you are faced with an even greater challenge. You have to introduce and explain any new concepts and define terms covered in the body.

Include one or more of the following in the introduction to help readers bridge the gap from the known to the unknown:

- A summary of related work that has already been accomplished on the topic in your company and possibly in other companies
- References to the sponsor(s)'s contract number, project title, internal sponsor(s), or similar other information
- General background on the topic

A good introduction should function much like the hook (HEY! YOU!) used in writing magazine articles: to entice the reader into reading the entire introduction and then the body.

If an introduction is too long, your reader may lose interest and quit.

The Body

Writing the body ("Tell them") of the report, the meat of your document, was covered in considerable detail in Chapter 9. Apply the techniques outlined there, and you'll have a well-formed body that is a pleasure to read.

Typically the body of a general report contains the following information:

1. More details about the problem
2. How others have attempted to solve it
3. Your attack plan
4. What you did to solve it
5. The results
6. What it proved or disproved

Conclusions

The conclusions module presents the most important findings or the results that follow logically from the body of the report. It gives a sense of completeness to a report by showing how the attack plan set up the solution to the problem stated in the introduction. Many readers will be more interested in the conclusions than in how the work was done.

The conclusions have already been outlined in the abstract but are covered here again ("Tell them what you told them") in more detail and with some justification. They should be brief (a paragraph or two for a short report and one or two pages for a long one), concise, to the point, and numbered. It's the numbering that helps make them brief, concise, and to the point.

Recommendations

Here you present your judgment about what should be done about the problem. Where does this lead? Where do we go from here? Based on and following the conclusions, the recommendations module examines the implications of the conclusions and renders an opinion on them—

for example, Is more study or investigation needed? Should the product studied be purchased or rejected? Should the project be considered completed? Should other approaches be considered?

Appendages

The appendix is a catchall that can include anything from complex mathematical derivations, to a host of data charts and tables, to reference documents, reports and contracts related to the subject of your report, and even a bibliography if you list many references.

Generally if only a few of the people reading your report require certain background or reference information, put this information in the appendix. If you're introducing many unfamiliar complex or technical terms throughout your writing, list them all alphabetically in a glossary so your readers can quickly locate the specific definition of each new term.

Designate appendixes with letters (Appendix A, Appendix B) and number the pages, figures, tables, equations, and other elements with the letter prefix (Figure A-1, etc.). Start each new appendix on a new page.

Longer reports deserve a comprehensive index to help locate specific topics. Indexes are relatively easy to prepare using modern word processing programs. One method used is to mark each individual key word in the text (a laborious process). A better procedure is to construct a concordance, a list of key words you want the index to cover. Using this concordance, the computer program will automatically search for and compile an index. An index prepared in this way will require some manual editing and verification, but at least the computer accomplishes about 95 percent of the task.

Report Writing Sequence

The following sequence is efficient and effective in writing a report:

1. Gather data.
2. Outline in detail before you start setting words in concrete.
3. Write the abstract so you'll know what the report is going to be about.
4. Write the introduction. Keep it short and to the point.
5. Write the body. Using your outline as a guide, write each module in any order you choose.

6. Write the conclusions and recommendations.
7. Prepare the appendixes. They contain material ancillary to the body.
8. Review and, if necessary, revise the abstract, introduction, body, conclusions, and recommendations.
9. Prepare the title page.
10. Prepare the contents, illustrations, and tables pages. List headings, subheadings, and figure and table numbers, along with page numbers.
11. Prepare the index.
12. Use the spelling checker and grammar checker.
13. Go to final copy.

Standard Report Formats

The use of standard formats for routine reports, whether they're pre-printed or adopted as company standards, has much to recommend it. They ensure that all the required information is provided, in the desired order and the desired format, and they enable readers to locate specific information easily. And it's always easier to complete a fill-in-the-blanks form than to write an open essay with no guidelines.

Periodic Activity Reports

A periodic activity report is management's basic method of monitoring groups and projects. It provides a record of the progress, the milestones met, the problems encountered and suggested solutions, additional facilities or personnel needed, the status of the program or project at a specific time, and the goals for the next period (Figure 11-2). The reporting period can range from a week to a month.

Each report refers to and carries on from the previous report, providing the continuity needed to monitor program progress. At the end of the program, the activity reports serve another valuable function: They form the basis for the final report that usually has to be written. It's difficult to remember all the details and activities of a long program and attempt to write a final report at the conclusion of the program unless the periodic activity reports are available.

Trip or Conference Report

Write trip and conference reports as soon as you can, when the material is still fresh in your memory. Explain the purposes and results of

Figure 11-2. Activity report form.

```
┌─────────────────────────────────────────┐
  Date:
  To:
  Copies to:
  From:                                              Introduction
  Project:
  Period Covered:
  Summary: [Use if report is over a page long]
└─────────────────────────────────────────┘


┌─────────────────────────────────────────┐
  Progress
      • Work accomplished during period
      • Problems encountered                          Body
      • Proposed solution(s)
      • Schedule (and budget?) status
└─────────────────────────────────────────┘


┌─────────────────────────────────────────┐
  Plans for Next Period                              Conclusion
└─────────────────────────────────────────┘
```

Figure 11-3. Trip or conference report form.

```
┌─────────────────────────────────────────┐
  Date:
  Distribution:
  Info Copies to:
  From:                                              Introduction
  Trip/Conference Personnel:
  Purpose of Trip:
  Summary: [If the report is over a page long]
└─────────────────────────────────────────┘


┌─────────────────────────────────────────┐
  Body:
      • Where and when did you go?
      • What did you do?                              Body
      • Who did you meet?
      • What did you learn?
└─────────────────────────────────────────┘


┌─────────────────────────────────────────┐
  Conclusion:
      • Any future action required?                   Conclusion
└─────────────────────────────────────────┘
```

Figure 11-4. Telephone conference report form.

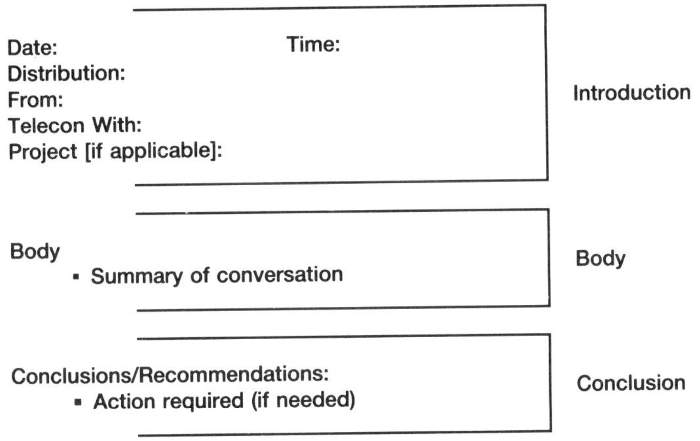

Date: Time:
Distribution:
From: Introduction
Telecon With:
Project [if applicable]:

Body   Body
  ▪ Summary of conversation

Conclusions/Recommendations: Conclusion
  ▪ Action required (if needed)

the trip or your attendance at a conference or convention (Figure 11-3). If you've made any customer contacts or uncovered any sales leads, mention them for follow-up, with copies to Marketing.

Telephone Conference Report

Often verbal agreements and commitments made over the telephone can come back to haunt you later on a program. After a telephone conference, document in a report any customer contacts made with the purchasing or contracts departments or with technical or management personnel (Figure 11-4).

12

The Manual

A manual is a set of written instructions for operating and or maintaining something—a process, for example, or equipment.

Operation manuals specify how to operate equipment or perform a process without explaining in detail how it functions. For example, an operation manual for a photocopier machine tells how to make copies, enlarge and reduce them, add toner, and so on, but it does not describe how the internal copying process works; for a word processing program, it outlines how to use the program, but it does not provide any computer or programming theory.

Maintenance manuals, on the other hand, must describe the theory of how equipment or processes function in enough detail so that the equipment or process can be fixed in case of failure and so preventive maintenance can be performed. An automotive repair and maintenance manual, for example, describes how the engine, transmission, and other components should function so that failures can be analyzed by checking for any deviation from normal operation. A TV and VCR repair and maintenance manual explains how signals are received and processed, lists possible problems that can occur, and describes tests to conduct to help a technician locate a fault and service it.

Often operation and maintenance are combined into a single manual. For example, a lawn mower manual describes how to operate the mower (hold handle and safety bar, how to adjust the blade, safety precautions to observe) and how to perform routine maintenance (change oil, clean the spark plug). A computer programming manual tells how a specific programming language (e.g., BASIC) functions and how to fix it (run and debug it) if it does not function properly or if updates need to be made.

Special Requirements

The Audience

The audience for manuals is large and broad, ranging from business professionals and scientists to technicians. Manuals must serve both ends of the spectrum—not boring skilled personnel at one end or confusing untrained users at the other extreme. This is a tall order.

Another factor complicates matters even more. Manual writers sometimes must write user-friendly manuals to compensate for equipment whose operating procedures are poorly designed, that is, equipment that is not user friendly. In other words, the manual writer must design and write the manual to compensate for this inadequacy by providing lengthy explanations of how to accomplish basic functions. Well-written software, for example, should lead the user through easy-to-follow, step-by-step procedures, preferably through the use of simple menus and easy-to-answer yes-or-no responses. Poorly written software requires that the operator learn and use numerous complex and often confusing computer commands.

One universal medium satisfies both extremes of the audience well: visuals. People often have widely different interpretations of what is written, and many complex concepts cannot be described with words alone. With illustrations, everyone sees the same pictures. Visuals are an important part of manuals that must address a wide spectrum of readers.

Some types of military specifications for manuals go so far as to specify that the contents of their technical manuals must be 75 percent illustration and only 25 percent text. This extreme approach is used for writing for military personnel who have only about a fifth-grade education.

Other techniques used when creating manuals designed for a broad spectrum of users are simple sentence construction, step-by-step instructions, lists, tables, logic trees, clear and informative titles, and physical divisions of modules.

Determine your audience before you top-down design. Does your audience include novices? laypersons? specialists? technicians? office secretaries? All of these?

Make a distribution list, by title, of the people who will read your manual. Jot down a few words about their backgrounds so you'll have a better picture of the people you will be addressing. Keep this audience foremost in your mind as you proceed with the design and writing.

The Imperative Mood

The key to writing clear and easy-to-understand procedures for manuals is the use of the imperative mood, as the following example effectively shows.

The boy, who afterward became General Wood, was once told by his grammar teacher, "Leonard, I will give you a sentence, and I want you to change it into the imperative mood. Here is the sentence: 'The horse draws the cart.' "

Young Wood quickly responded, "Giddap!"

See how effective and word saving the imperative mood is?

When writing instructions, use the imperative mood. Instead of writing, "The knob should be turned to the extreme right," use "Turn the knob to the extreme right." After you've written the instructions, dry-run the procedure or action yourself, following your written instructions to make certain they work as written.

Logic Trees

Users often must make specific decisions when performing an operation or when inputting or outputting information. If prose is used to describe a series of operations, the user has to remember all the decisions made earlier—often a difficult task because some operating sequences can be quite lengthy and complex.

In a properly designed manual, this decision process should be made easy to understand so that all the user has to do is make simple yes-or-no decisions about a limited series of questions or sentences to arrive at a solution. The procedure should also be designed so that the user does not have to remember the previous decisions. A technique that accomplishes these objectives is the logic tree, illustrated in the simplified example of Figure 12-1.

Logic trees may take up much more space than text; however, properly designed, they are a hundred times easier to understand than straight prose. A logic tree should have mostly yes-or-no questions and can branch off into many subbranches.

Locating Information

Since manuals are seldom read from cover to cover, you have to make it easy for readers to find the information they need. For example, a user may only want to learn how to format a computer disk without

Figure 12-1. Logic tree for photocopier troubleshooting.

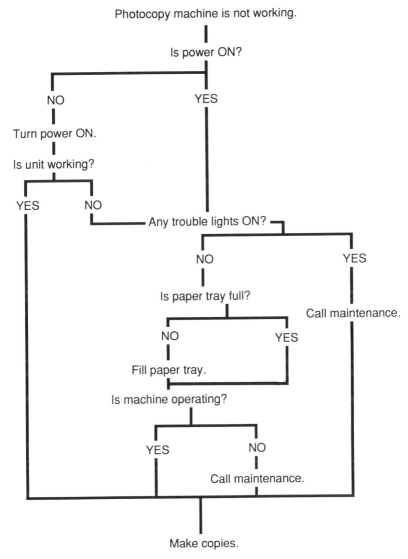

having to suffer through a long dissertation on disk drives and disk storage formats. Users are impatient and need quick answers. Here are some suggestions on how you can help readers locate a desired module quickly:

▪ In the summary, state what is included in the document and where to find it.

▪ At the beginning of each chapter, include a block outline of the chapter's contents.

▪ Provide comprehensive lists of contents, illustrations, and tables. A well-constructed index is an excellent aid. If possible, use tabs to help locate key modules.

▪ Use redundancy. When a user seeks to learn about an operation, he or she does not want to continually flip pages back and forth (in computer jargon, they are called "go to's") to read interrelated background information. Many modules of the manual should be able to stand alone, even if the result is considerable redundancy.

▪ Use descriptive, informative titles for all chapters, headings, visuals, and tables (e.g., instead of "Disk Drive," use "Loading Your Disk Drive")

▪ Establish different font sizes for different topic levels—one size for chapter titles, a smaller size for module headings—so the importance of each level is immediately obvious.

▪ Highlight important information by italics, underlining, boxes, and other devices.

▪ Present information in easy-to-understand formats (tables, visuals, boxes, lists).

▪ Use the chapter number as a prefix for pages, figure and table numbers, and modules (e.g., Chapter 3 pages are numbered 3-1, 3-2, etc.). Designate each module by a numbered heading (e.g., 3.3 "How to Format a Disk"). This makes information easier to find and the module easier to update. And if different versions, options, or models of a basic equipment or software are produced (such as using most of the same basic manual for both IBM and Macintosh computers), numbering a manual in this fashion simplifies creating manuals for a variety of computer models.

Manual Design From the Top Down

If you already have a format to follow, skip the procedure outlined in Figure 12-1. But, if you have the freedom to create your own chapter topics and titles, this procedure will show you how.

Chapter Design

Selecting Title, Purpose, and Theme

Begin by choosing a title that is an informative, brief summary of the precise function of the manual—for example, "User Manual for Word Perfect 5.1," "Operation Manual for IBM AT," or "Operation and Maintenance Manual—Delta FAX Machine—Model XTA1." (Chapter 10 contains a thorough discussion on choosing a title.)

Brainstorming and Conducting Preliminary Research

Your goal in this step is to view your overall manual from a high-level perspective and create chapter titles for its main divisions. This part of the design will be mostly a surface look, without delving into too much detail. For this step, think big.

The amount of brainstorming and preliminary research required depends on where you're starting from. If you have adequate notes and references, and you already know a great deal about the subject, this step may have already been accomplished. If, however, you're starting from zero and have little or no direction on what to write, you may need to invest considerable effort here.

If you have no outline or no specific format to follow, begin by brainstorming. Sit down and relax with a set of note cards and a pen, and start making notes on what you think should be included in the manual. Don't judge your thoughts; write everything down. This is a preliminary step; you can't decide how applicable your material will be until you begin to evaluate the complete set of notes that you have accumulated for each module.

Once your brainstorming is completed, begin conducting preliminary research. First check within your company to determine if any previous manuals have been written on similar topics. If so, make a note of the chapter titles, the format used, the size, number of pages, illustration types, and so on. Then visit the company and/or public library to find material on the subject. Review it and make appropriate notes.

Creating Chapters and Titles

Review the information you have accumulated during brainstorming and preliminary research with the objective of creating chapter divisions and titles. Or review the suggested formats included later in this chapter to see if one applies to your material.

The possible choices for chapter divisions are not too great since the functions of most manuals are typically well defined and limited. You're going to have to cover such fundamental topics as how to unpack and set up the equipment (if applicable); how to turn it on and adjust or set it up for operation; what the various modes of operation are; how to input, control, and output information; and what to do if the equipment is not operating properly. A list of common error messages and their repair procedures must be included as well as reference information, such as the serial numbers, size and capacity of the equipment, and perhaps an exploded-view drawing that shows how to order replacement or optional parts.

The balance of the steps in Figure 12–2—sorting material into chapters, organizing and ordering chapters, and updating the outline—were explored thoroughly in Chapters 8 and 9.

Module Design

The procedure required to design the individual modules for each chapter is similar to that for chapter design. It is outlined in Figure 12-3.

Writing the Modules

The procedure for writing modules from the bottom up is illustrated in Figure 12-4 and has been covered in Chapters 8, 9, and 11. Only the last step has not been already covered.

The front and back matter are important components since manuals are rarely read from beginning to end. Users scan a manual and use it basically as a reference to locate specific items of interest, so you must provide a number of road maps to help them. In the front matter are the preface (and acknowledgments), contents, illustrations, and tables. The back matter can contain appendixes, an index, and a bibliography.

 • The *preface* (also known as an introduction or summary) should state the name and composition of the equipment or process (IBM AT with 2 Megs of RAM, one 3.5-inch floppy, and one hard disk drive), the version it covers (DOS software version 5.0), and which auxiliary

Figure 12-2. Chapter design for a manual.

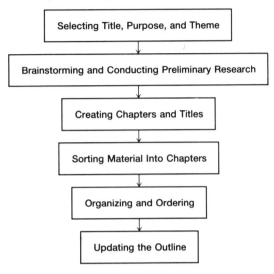

Figure 12-3. Module design for a manual.

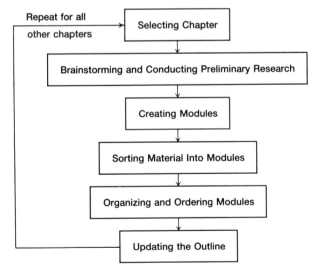

Figure 12-4. Module writing procedure for manuals.

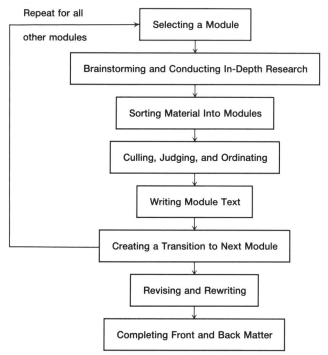

equipment it functions with (laser printer required). It should also summarize how the manual is organized ("This manual is divided into four sections as follows:") and how to use it ("Decide which options you wish to install, and refer to the appropriate sections"). If a number of individuals have been involved in planning and writing the manual, their contributions can be acknowledged here or in a separate acknowledgments section if the list is extensive. A copyright statement is also needed near the front of the manual.

▪ Place the *Contents* just after the title page, followed by a list of figures and tables. The lists should be comprehensive and indented to show subordination of topics. All of the modules and pages should be numbered by chapter (e.g., 3-1, 3-2). The contents of each chapter should appear at the start of the chapter.

▪ *Appendixes* include information required for only some users, such as a theoretical discussion of telecommunications for an on-line system that would only be read by skilled users. The glossary contains an alphabetical list of all the new terms introduced in the manual, along with easy-to-understand definitions.

 ▪ If the manual has over about thirty-five pages, provide a comprehensive index. Err on the side of including too many references rather than too few.

 ▪ For some manuals, a *bibliography* may have to be included if certain users need to be referred to other documents for further information. A bibliography of helpful references is especially useful when the audience has a wide range of backgrounds and skills.

Manual Outlines

General Manual

Although manual formats may differ from product to product and company to company, their basic content is very similar. The following format is useful for a broad range of manuals:

Front matter. In addition to the usual front matter, other items that might be included in this section, depending on the type of equipment or software, are warranty policies, license policy, copyright information, a listing of trademarks, and any special notices, such as an escape clause: "We reserve the right to revise this publication without the obligation to notify any person of such changes."

Chapter 1: General Information. Provide the system specifications, briefly describe the equipment, and summarize the operation of the equipment or software. This is a summary that most users will read, so it should deal primarily with general topics that apply to all users.

Chapter 2: Instructions for Use. Detail the operation of the equipment or software and describe the varied modes of operation—how to control, modify, and input and output information. This chapter will receive more use than all the rest of the chapters combined.

Chapter 3: Maintenance. List error messages for a software program, and provide instructions on how to correct the errors. For equipment, detail the procedures for performing routine preventive and corrective maintenance, overhaul and repair procedures, parts lists, an exploded view if needed, circuit and logic diagrams, and other similar information.

Chapter 4: Installation. Chapter 4 will probably be used only once, so it should be out of the way of normal use, placed near the back of the manual. For software, prescribe the setup procedures required to let your software program know what type of monitor and printer you have, what options you want to exercise, and so forth. For hardware, cover such topics as the physical space, mounting and power requirements, unpacking the equipment and setting it up, and necessary adjustments.

Other chapters. Chapters may be added to discuss other subjects not covered earlier (e.g., adding special printers to a software program, describing optional equipment available, alternate modes of operation).

Back matter. The back matter contains ancillary material as needed— for example, a bibliography or glossary.

Equipment Operations and Maintenance Manual

Here's a suggested outline for an operations and maintenance manual for equipment.

Chapter 1:—General Information. Relay to readers basic information about the equipment—for example, a brief explanation of its capabilities, model numbers and serial numbers covered in the manual, vital statistics (size, weight, power requirements), and its relation to other equipment it operates with. This chapter serves as an executive summary and is directed toward a wide readership.

Chapter 2: Operation. Chapter 2 will be used more than any other part of the manual. Detail the procedures to turn on, set up, and operate the equipment; supply photos and/or drawings of all controls, switches, adjustments, and so forth needed during normal operation; and specify safety requirements, warnings and cautions, operational checks, emergency operation, and turn-off procedures.*

Chapter 3: Functional Description. This part of the manual describes how the equipment operates from a theoretical standpoint; it often has to be written with close consultation with and review by many technical experts. It typically includes mechanical, block, logic, and circuit

---

*A *warning* refers to conditions, practices, or procedures that must be observed to avoid personal injury, loss of life, or a long-term health hazard. A *caution* refers to conditions, practices, or procedures that must be observed to avoid damage to equipment or destruction of equipment. *Notes* provide essential information of special importance or interest or that which will aid in job performance.

diagrams of the top assembly and of as many subassemblies as are required.

Chapter 4: Scheduled [or Preventive] Maintenance. Most equipment requires some scheduled preventive maintenance to keep it functioning properly. This important chapter covers the periodic inspections, cleaning, adjustments, calibration, and self-tests required to avert future problems.

Chapter 5: Troubleshooting. Sooner or later all equipment—whether it's a computer, a forklift, or a toaster—fails to operate properly. Outline the basic troubleshooting procedures required to isolate the cause(s) of the most common faults and repair them.

Chapter 6: Corrective Maintenance. Specify the disassembly and assembly procedures required to access, remove, and replace a faulty part or component in the unit. Exploded views, along with text describing the step-by-step disassembly and assembly procedures, are vital.

Chapter 7: Parts Lists. Supply detailed parts lists, often accompanied by exploded views that illustrate all the major replacement parts, their locations, part numbers, and other relevant information.

Chapter 8: Installation. Some manuals place installation information in Chapter 1 or 2. I believe that since installation is usually a one-time procedure, and once performed need not be referred to again, the information belongs near the back, where it won't clutter up the early important chapters. For equipment mounted in a fixed site, provide diagrams of the mounting requirements and procedures, the hookup, the operating environment, plus any special tests required in the initial installation of the unit. Any special instructions for unpacking and packing the equipment or storage requirements belong here, as do any preoperational checks, calibration, and adjustments required before the unit is turned on for the first time.

Tutorial Manual

Tutorials are written or programmed instruction courses to teach users how to use an equipment or software program or perform a process or a procedure. They provide step-by-step instructions, requiring user interaction in conducting actual operations or in replying to questions. In a truly interactive tutorial, if a user answers a questions incorrectly, the tutorial should provide some branching to supply extra assistance and extra tests to clarify the topic. The best tutorials should teach the user not only the correct method for performing certain operations but should also build in and demonstrate some representative incorrect responses so the user can learn how errors occur and how to recover from them.

Follow this recommended outline:

Chapter 1: Introduction. Begin by summarizing the course of instruction. For a hands-on tutorial, the introduction also includes as a minimum information on:

- The equipment and/or software required
- How the course is organized
- How long the course will take to complete
- How to pause in the course and start again
- How to recover from user input errors
- Any special suggestions on performing the tutorial

Chapter 2: Operation. Organize this chapter on a known-to-unknown order—beginning with what the user knows, perhaps reviewing some background information, and then providing some simple exercises. Hands-on tutoring is by far the best method to learn a subject.

Other Chapters. If the operation is broken down into a number of major modes, perhaps a new chapter should be devoted to each major mode. For example, a graphic software program could devote one chapter of a tutorial showing how to use and modify standard figures, such as circles or squares; another chapter could be devoted to methods for free drawing unique symbols and curves.

Appendixes. One or more appendixes can be used for such topics as error messages, new terms, background material, special and unique modes of operation, reference information such as advanced tutorials or a bibliography, and an index.

PC Manual

A personal computer (PC) manual covers the basic operation of a computer but usually has little or no information on its internal workings. To operate a personal computer, you don't necessarily have to know the difference between a 1 and a 0 or even what the word *binary* means. Most of these details have been taken care of by the talented programmers who correctly shield the users from this unnecessary detail and supply them with well-designed, easy-to-use menus.

Here's a recommended general outline for a PC manual:

Introduction. Summarize the basic features of the PC, and specify its capacity, model number, and version if applicable. This section can often be used as a subtle sales pitch promoting the computer.

Chapter 1: Summary. Most users will read this chapter from beginning to end, so be concise, direct it to a diverse audience, summarize the content of the manual, and describe how to learn how to operate the equipment.

Chapter 2: Basic Components. Discuss the various major components that comprise the computer, include photos or drawings of each major component, and explain their basic purposes from a user standpoint. Explain the basic functions of the extra keyboard keys and how to use them. Describe how to care for the basic components (e.g., "Keep disks away from magnetic sources") and how to perform such fundamental operations as turning the unit on and off and formatting a disk.

Chapter 3: How It Works. This chapter starts out by assuming that the computer is booted up, disks have been formatted, and the computer is ready to accomplish some useful functions. It focuses on system operation, starting from a root directory and moving on to the basic functions that can be performed from the root directory prompt or a basic menu. It also explains the method for loading and using special software and methods for inputting, saving, and printing data.

Other Chapters. A number of other chapters can be included to cover other special aspects of the computer's operation, among them the following:

- *Unpacking the System:* This can be included as an appendix or a later chapter in the manual since it will only be used once. Include illustrations and a pictorial inventory of the system components.
- *Setting up the Computer:* The instructions tell how the computer must be set up, with detailed drawings and/or photos. This section belongs in a later chapter since it explains a one-time procedure.
- *Other Major Modes of Operation:* Additional chapters can be devoted to any other major modes of operation (such as an editing mode) that are available.

- *Adding More Options to Your PC:* Most PCs are designed for low cost and consequently provide only a basic capability. But most are also designed to have excellent expansion potential so that options can be added later with a minimum of modification, such as installing a plug-in module. Additional memory, a serial port, an internal clock, and more floppy drives are some of these options. A chapter devoted to describing some of the more common options is another subtle sales pitch.
- *Programming Basics:* Depending on the nature of the PC, some version of the BASIC programming language should be described so that knowledgeable users can program and tailor some simple functions. A chapter could be devoted to the elements of programming in a BASIC language and also perhaps briefly outline other possible programming languages.
- *Help and Troubleshooting:* A chapter devoted to helping users learn how to troubleshoot the most common faults or misadventures caused by errors in operation and manipulation and to determine how to fix them is essential. Direct the material to cover users with a wide variety of backgrounds, address the most common problems, and suggest easy-to-understand and simple-to-perform solutions. An alphabetical or numerical list of possible error messages is particularly useful.
- *Glossary:* An extensive list of new terms introduced in the manual with simple definitions is essential.
- *Bibliography:* List additional texts and manuals that explore in depth other aspects of the PC's operation. For example, some users may wish to learn in greater depth how to program in the FORTRAN language or connect to a computer network.

Software Manual

A software manual describes how a particular software program should be installed and used on specific computer types. If operation of the program is virtually self-explanatory for experienced users, a special section in the front could be included and designated, "Quick Start for the Experienced User." This quick start should not be more than a page or two with instructions on how to set up and start the software. The balance of the manual typically can be organized according to the following format:

Introduction. List the computer models the program will function on and the requirements of that computer, state the software version, and describe the general operation of the software.

Chapter 1: General. Describe the basic capabilities of the program, the basic specifications it meets, and, briefly, the operating modes.

Chapter 2: Operation. Most software programs start with a menu that lists the basic functions that can be performed. This chapter should work its way down the menu, detailing how to activate the various functions, what they do, and how to use them. A help menu should be available at all times, no matter what mode is being used, providing an alphabetical listing of functions that describes what they do and a supplemental short description of how they're activated. It should also be easy to get into and out of the help menu.

Other Chapters:

- *Tutorial:* Some of the more complex software programs have a built-in interactive tutorial stored on the program disks. The manual should summarize this tutorial, list the subjects, tell how long it takes to complete it, and instruct how to get into and out of it.
- *Other Major Modes of Operation:* If any other major modes of operation are possible, additional chapters can be devoted to them.

Whatever Happened to the HEY! YOU! SEE? SO!

A user manual is written for a human, not for a machine. The HEY! is the title of the manual, the hard cover, the method used to bind it (spiral or looseleaf is preferred), the colors, and attention-grabbing type on the cover. The YOU! should be prominent in the instructions. Use the magic word *you* rather than *the user* to personalize your instructions.

There should be plenty of SEE? or instructions in the manual on how to use a software program, equipment, or a procedure. The SO! is implied in the use of the manual. When the user has learned how to use the computer or a complex software program, the SO!, or the "Ah so!" is happily uttered in satisfaction.

Manuals in the Future

Even now, some of the more elementary manuals are being delivered as text stored on the same disk as the software program. Usually these are stored as ASCII text so that any basic word processor can display it. The user can read the manual by displaying the text on the screen or printing it out for a hard copy. This saves the time and expense of publishing and distributing a paper manual. Disk storage provides a medium that can be quickly updated by simply editing and issuing new disks to the users.

There are, however, some distinct disadvantages to this approach. The ability to present high-quality visuals is extremely limited, and color visuals are even more limited. Users are not accustomed to reading a monitor screen instead of a paper copy. Moreover, a hard copy permits quick scanning back and forth.

But technology continues to create leapfrogging solutions to these problems. One of the most promising techniques is the use of compact disks (CDs), which have the capability to store not only text and visuals but also a voice track that can expand on the visuals and the text. The future holds great promise for new and revolutionary changes in the manner in which future manuals will be created and delivered. All business professionals must learn how to use these new media.

These incredible advances in media will not, however, accomplish the task of automatically writing manuals. Research, organization, writing, and rewriting will still be essential parts of our daily business activities. All revolutionary technology accomplishes is to provide new media for communicating information and to take some of the drudgery out of the task. Modern technology is useless without people who can write and communicate clearly, accurately, and effectively.

13

The Proposal

I Corinthians 9:24 reads: "Do you not know that those who race in the stadium all run, to be sure, but one receives the prize? So, run your race that you may win it." This race has been going on for centuries, and it is true that whoever has the best proposal will win the race.

A proposal is a sales document designed to sell a potential customer on the ability of the proposing company to supply a product or a service. It's a competitive offer, a plan of action for fulfilling a need. Most proposals are for the procurement of nonstandard items or for the purchase of services. It thus explains how a problem can be solved, the equipment and/or personnel required, and the cost and time schedule needed for completion. Many in business, science, education, industry, engineering, and government use proposals as the primary tool for acquiring new business, establishing new product lines, and creating new opportunities.

The proposal is often a highly complex and expensive document to design and write. It is used not only to obtain business from other companies but also to obtain approval for in-house company projects. The range covered is enormous. I've participated in proposals ranging in size from a single-page letter proposal for a one-week task to a proposal for a new avionics system that occupied over a hundred management and engineering personnel for an entire year and resulted in a ten-foot-high stack of multivolumed documents.

Most business writing deals with items that exist. A proposal, however, deals with items that will be accomplished in the future; thus, it must be written in a convincing manner, adequately describing a result or object that may exist only as an idea in the proposer's imagination. It must be developed logically in a step-by-step manner that shows how the problem will be solved. The proposal must persuade the reader(s) that the approach is not only valid but the best solution with the winning edge over the competition. Dividing the proposal up into modules and using the Precedent Sort to organize these modules into a logical sequence helps meet these stringent requirements.

Another important writing consideration is that the same proposal must satisfy not only business personnel but also the management, purchasing, and operating staffs. Thus, sections of it must be written in easy-to-understand language for personnel of widely different backgrounds.

We live in an age of high technology and high competition. Purchasing decisions are becoming increasingly complex. The number of purchase options available is multiplying so rapidly that an individual can no longer order equipment by a simple part number. You can't just decide to order a computer; you have to specify how much memory, what types of plug-in modules you need, the number and types of ports, the printer type and model. More and more RFPs (requests for proposal) are required in lieu of part numbers to specify and purchase specialty items and services. The proposal is rapidly becoming the primary medium for managing this diverse variety of procurements.

Types of Proposals

Proposals can be written to solve a variety of existing or anticipated problems.

- *Feasibility Study.* A feasibility study evaluates how one or more alternative approaches can solve a problem. For example, a feasibility study could examine and evaluate the desirability of moving a company's facilities from a crowded urban location to a remote, less costly, rural site.

- *Research Grant.* The field of research grants covers a wide range of proposals, from astronomy to zoology. Research grants are usually awarded to academic, scholarly, or think-tank types of institutions to investigate a theory, an idea, or a phenomenon to determine what caused it and whether it can be of practical use or to determine if investigating it will simply contribute to the general knowledge about the subject. Research grants are vital to a country's future, even if 98 percent of them do not bring about positive results. That tiny 2 percent overwhelmingly justifies the expenditure for all the unsuccessful grants.

- *In-Company Proposals.* Most companies have provision for their employees to submit their ideas to management for consideration, often giving cash rewards to the successful. These proposals may range from a single page to a multipage document. In-company proposals may be solicited or unsolicited. They may deal with suggested improvements in company management or procedures.

- *Internal Research and Development.* Another excellent source of development money is IR&D funds that companies budget to finance product ideas and development programs that their employees have come up with, such as a proposal for a new software program.

- *Procurement of New Equipment.* Companies that are not skilled in engineering new technologies (e.g., a grocery store) must make complex decisions in determining what type of new equipment to purchase (bar code reader) and what options to add (tie in to store-computer inventory system). These decisions can cost millions of dollars in investment and require radical changes in operations and management. To help make these vital decisions, companies hire outside consultants, who must write a proposal that demonstrates an intimate knowledge of the new technology—its practicality and advantages and disadvantages—and prove that they are totally unbiased in their evaluation of competitive equipment.

- *Sales Plan.* To remain successful in business, companies must keep selling. A sales plan addresses this issue. A proposal for a sales plan can cover the many aspects of increasing sales: increased advertising (direct mail, newspapers, etc.), customer surveys (what do you like or not like about our product?), different packaging (bright colors, bolder lettering), and other techniques. A sales proposal is usually written by a creative person on the sales force or an outside consultant skilled in these matters.

- *Product or Business Plan.* Before a new product is developed and marketed, a proposal should be prepared that describes the product or business plan. This proposal establishes goals, specifications for the product, a budget and a schedule, and the company facilities and personnel required to develop the product. This plan should extend all the way through the marketing phase, including how the product will be packaged and promoted and its sales potential.

- *Services.* Few companies have all the skills required to keep pace with the complex developments of new technology, so they must hire consultants or contract workers to assist them. For some projects, companies wisely choose to hire temporary workers to help with peak loads. The consultants or contract workers responding to this need must prepare a proposal that will delineate the services to be performed, the facilities needed, the cost, the schedule, and supporting data that document their particular expertise.

▪ *Plan for Change.* One constant fact in the business profession is change: new facilities, a move to a new area, purchase of new equipment. A major change, such as installing a new and costly computer system, must be preceded by a detailed proposal that outlines the mechanics of the change, the effects it will have on day-to-day activities and on the workers, the new or modified facilities required, the cost and schedule, and other affected parameters.

▪ *Development Program.* One of the most common types of equipment proposal is to develop a product to meet certain specifications. This product may be hardware, software, or services. A proposal for a development program responds directly to the applicable specs by evaluating various approaches and selecting an approach that the proposer concludes is optimum. The proposal also includes a development plan, a schedule, and the projected costs. How the program will be managed and which specific company personnel will be assigned to the project are important proposal inputs. This type of program often provides an excellent opportunity for a company to enter a new field of endeavor or to improve its existing equipment or software product lines.

▪ *Production Program.* Some companies lack the skills or facilities required to manufacture equipment they have developed, so they must locate a company to produce the equipment to meet original company specifications. A proposal for a production program dwells heavily on the proposer's facilities, production and quality control procedures, and ability to meet the desired schedule and cost. Examples of success on similar programs are particularly helpful.

Four tenses are commonly used in proposal writing:

1. Past tense
2. Present tense
3. Future tense
4. Pretense

To write winning proposals, your task is to use only the first three tenses and minimize the last.

General Requirements

At a minimum, the proposal should include:

- A clear statement of the problem as it is understood by the proposer and a discussion of the background of the problem.

- A discussion of alternate approaches to solving the problem and the advantages and disadvantages of each one.

- An explanation of which approach will be used and how it will solve the problem.

- A milestone schedule, the estimated cost of the program and justification for the cost, a management plan, facilities available, and a list of personnel to be involved, along with their resumes.

A proposal should be about half sales-pitch (some say 90 percent) and half problem solving. But remember that a proposal addresses professional people, so a high-pressure sales pitch will work to one's disadvantage.

The goal of a well-written proposal is to convince the potential sponsor that your company can perform a specific job better than all your competitors. If your company receives the subsequent contract, the proposal then becomes part of a binding contract when it is accepted, or it can be offered as a basis for future negotiations. Both the proposer and the sponsor try to protect their interests to the full extent of the law, so it's important that a proposal strike a proper balance between promising to accomplish too much and meeting the minimum proposal requirements.

Proposal Response Steps

The steps required to prepare for and to respond to a proposal are outlined in Figure 13-1. Proposals can be written for either solicited or unsolicited procurements. For a solicited proposal, the procedure is fairly formal and well defined. The unsolicited proposal, however, results when someone (or some company) has an idea and searches for a company or group to sponsor that idea. For an unsolicited proposal, some of the steps in Figure 13-1 are eliminated. For example, a bidders' conference would not be held and a bid–no bid decision has presumably already been made unless internal approval is required to invest company funds in the proposal effort.

Usually only a limited time is available to respond to an RFP. For this reason, a significant investment in time and effort during the pre-proposal phase is highly advantageous. And a well-planned and scheduled proposal response cycle is a necessity to ensure a complete

Figure 13-1. Procedure for designing and writing a proposal.

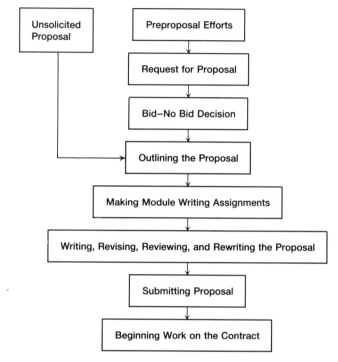

and credible response to the varied document requirements. Nonresponsive proposals are often written on a panic schedule, with excessive overtime being required of its participants, usually because of poor planning by management. Working to an overtime schedule for an extended period lowers efficiency and can all but kill the creativity and initiative that are so vital to success. Detailed planning, a realistic schedule, and adhering closely to this plan and schedule considerably increase the chances for a proposal's success.

Preproposal Efforts

Whether the proposal is solicited or unsolicited, a preproposal effort expended far in advance of a formal proposal request pays substantial dividends in responding to the proposal. The more preproposal effort you invest, the easier it is to write the proposal and the better are your chances for winning. Often an intensive preproposal effort can result in the early completion of a preliminary design for the proposal and a detailed plan for meeting the requirements, giving you a head start on responding to the RFP. In many cases, an intensive preproposal effort is essential even to be included on the bidders' list.

Much of the proposal documentation can be prepared ahead of time: descriptions of company facilities, personnel résumés, company administration policies, company experience, management policies, and others. The precise format the RFP requires may be changed, but if you have all the raw information stored on computer disks, it's easy to reformat and adapt to the RFP's specific requirements. Prepare as much of this boilerplate material ahead of time as possible so you can devote your principal effort to the specific design, writing, and cost-estimating requirements of the RFP.

Unless you have great insight into a sponsor's problems, the likelihood of obtaining funding for an unsolicited proposal is not great. Since researching and writing an unsolicited proposal require a significant investment, initial contact should be made to a potential sponsor in the form of a query letter, two or three pages in length, that describes the proposed activity, shows how it is of value to the potential sponsor, and describes the facilities and equipment needed and those already on hand. Provide an estimate of the time required to perform the effort. Estimated cost is not appropriate at the query level since the program cannot be adequately defined until the sponsor responds. Finally, offer to supply a full-length proposal tailored to the sponsor's specific requirements.

The first step in a preproposal effort begins with planning and strategy meetings in your company (or by yourself for a one-person proposal) and possible visits with the potential sponsor(s) of the work. Much in-depth information on a customer can be obtained from the open literature. The sponsor's organization can be researched in existing documentation, as well as its products and the markets it serves. Considerable other information can be obtained from trade shows, business and technical publications, on-line databases, and professional and industrial associations, such as the American Management Association.

This preproposal period is an opportune time to determine the sponsor's problems and major concerns by personally meeting with the sponsor's management and personnel. You can learn the sponsor's biases and possibly the preferred approaches to the sponsor's problems. This preliminary effort is very important because it can help steer the RFP in such a manner that it will favor or be slanted toward your design or your approach. For an unsolicited proposal, you may even have an opportunity to help your customer write the RFP and the accompanying specifications. This can result in your being in a favored position or even of being awarded a contract on a highly desirable, noncompetitive basis—a sole-source award.

Another source of sponsor and competitor information has been made possible by the Freedom of Information Act. You can demand a copy of any government contract (subject to security restrictions and, to a limited extent, company proprietary information), which will provide information about your competitors—their costing, performance rating, and so on. This is an excellent method of evaluating your competitive position.

The preproposal effort you invest in planning, obtaining competitive information, meeting with the customer, creating preliminary design concepts, accumulating boilerplate material, and initiating an earlier start will provide you with an excellent competitive edge.

Request for Proposal

RFPs typically contain three sections:

1. *General information section:* Includes the general instructions for responding to the RFP, a cover sheet, and a brief technical description.

2. *Boilerplate:* Describes standard information the sponsor delivers with each RFP, including standard forms the proposer needs to fill out, inspection and acceptance requirements, packaging and marking, deliveries and performance, and a complete list of applicable documents.

3. *Instructions:* The heart of the RFP that sets out the detailed instructions for the preparation of the proposal: the format desired (including the sequence of topics to be covered); the statement of work (SOW), detailing the specific tasks to be accomplished under the contract; the contract data requirements list (CDRL), listing the data (progress reports, production drawings, software documentation, source code, final report) to be supplied as part of the contract and the corresponding delivery schedule; and the proposal evaluation criteria, listing the key factors (experience, technical approach, facilities, personnel) that the sponsor will judge to evaluate your proposal.

Often a single specification—call it the product spec—is used as the main procurement spec. This product spec is referenced by the SOW and imposes a number of specs that must be applied to the procurement. The product spec describes in detail the requirements the proposer has to meet and the extent to which the applicable specs apply. It should also detail testing and acceptance procedures for the product or the service.

To initiate the formal proposal cycle, an RFP is issued to all qualified companies on the bidders' list. The potential bidders are then given a short period, perhaps two to four weeks, to review the RFP requirements; then they meet with the sponsor to resolve any questions, or the sponsor may request that the bidders formally submit their questions in writing. The sponsor then sends the questions, along with the answers, to all the bidders to ensure equitable treatment for all.

Bid–No Bid Decision

With their questions answered, the bidders individually decide if they wish to pursue bidding on the contract by holding a bid–no bid meeting. This important decision must not be arrived at too hastily since individuals and companies that respond must decide whether to invest a significant amount of their money, facilities, personnel, and time in replying to an RFP. However, a company cannot procrastinate too long in making the decision; the time available for responding to the RFP is severely limited.

One of the most important factors to consider is your or your company's competitive position with respect to the other bidders. If the competition is substantial, well financed, and aggressive, highly innovative approaches are required.

As far as the cost investment required to write a proposal, one rule of thumb is that an investment of about 1 percent of the gross value of the contract for one year is reasonable. Thus, if a contract has a potential of $1 million in the first year, a proposal investment of about $10,000 is considered reasonable. Other factors, such as the desire to enter a new field or market in a new geographical area or to improve one's products or services, can motivate a company to invest a substantially higher percentage.

Assuming a bid decision has been made, the bidder must assemble a proposal team, appoint a proposal manager and staff, and outline and schedule the proposal effort in considerable detail. The work to be performed on the contract is described in the SOW and is often mapped out in a work breakdown structure (WBS) (Figure 13-2). The WBS, much like an organization chart, divides the overall job into bite-sized, individual work modules or tasks. A proposal manager should head the entire project and appoint managers for the basic work divisions.

Each work module, designated by a number, covers a specific part of the overall program that must be accomplished. Even for a one-

Figure 13-2. Work breakdown structure.

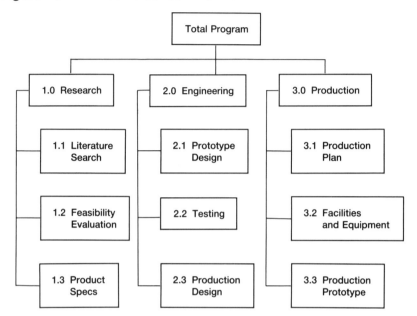

person effort, the WBS is a recommended approach because it provides a good basic organization for estimating costs and helps ensure that all the requirements of the RFP will be responded to.

The primary function of a WBS is to document and specify the work modules so that the personnel and material to be expended on the program can be identified, estimated, justified, and scheduled. Here again a program is designed from the top down using a WBS, then cost estimated and scheduled from the bottom up.

In the example shown in Figure 13-2, the WBS is designed from the top down to create the individual work modules. Then the cost is arrived at by estimating the cost required to complete the Literature Search (1.1), Feasibility Evaluation (1.2), and the Product Specs (1.3) efforts. These three work modules are then added to build up to the Research (1.0) effort. Finally, all the work modules are summed up, along with the management and other costs, to estimate the cost of the entire program.

The WBS does not directly apply to writing the text of the proposal. It is used primarily for costing and scheduling a proposed program. But the text for the proposal must be written in parallel because the same individuals who estimate the work modules must also write the corresponding text that informs the sponsor how the specific tasks will be accomplished. The WBS and the proposal text must be closely integrated.

Outlining the Proposal

Now the real work begins. The proposal manager and staff create a detailed outline of the proposal—one that accounts for all the work modules and matches the corresponding text modules with the corresponding WBS work modules. These text modules are assigned to the personnel who are estimating the work modules so that the task and schedule correspond precisely with the analysis and recommendations of the proposal.

Creating a detailed outline is probably the most important step in the entire proposal cycle because the text and the accompanying illustrations, along with the cost, are the key factors that will win or lose the contract. If the text and visuals do not convince the proposal evaluators that you or your company is the best qualified for the job, your effort has been wasted. This is a one-time effort to obtain a particular contract. You are not going to be given the opportunity to retract part of your proposal and say, "What I really meant to say was . . ."

Make a considerable investment in time, managerial talent, and professionals to design, organize, review, and revise the proposal content to guarantee the best efforts. Use brainstorming and everyone's creative powers to come up with ideas, thoughts, and alternative solutions. Then use the Precedent Sort to give order to the ideas, devise an outline, and create the text modules. Add effective visuals to supplement and make the text easier to write. Finally write, review, rewrite, revise, and rewrite the best proposal that the combined efforts of a team of dedicated professionals can come up with.

A careful analysis must be made of the proposal specifications to determine the special emphasis that a sponsor places on certain aspects of the RFP problems. This will let you know what the sponsor believes are the most important and most difficult problems that have to be solved. Use this information to address the specific concerns in the proposal.

Making Module Writing Assignments

If the proposal is small, it is relatively easy to ensure that the appropriate personnel are assigned and that the effort will be well coordinated. For large proposals, with several authors assigned to research and write different text modules of a proposal, special problems exist. Duplication can occur when different writers discuss the same problems; they may even come up with different—and noncompatible—solutions. Writing styles of different writers may be so radically different that the sponsor will be so severely jolted in reading the proposal that continuity and believability, two vital characteristics of successful proposals, will suffer.

Investing in a concerted effort in creating, directing all writers to follow a detailed outline, and maintaining close coordination of the work will help solve some of the problems. Use of a single editor or senior technical writer to supervise the organization and to review and edit all writers' contributions will help create some much-needed consistency in style and content.

Writing, Revising, Reviewing, and Rewriting the Proposal

Although proposals for different programs may differ in subject and size, their content is pretty much the same. Certain basic information must be included, whether for a one-page or multivolume proposal or for hardware or services.

The cost section (or volume) of the proposal is a complex subject and will not be covered here (although Appendix 13B describes some of the types of contract funding available). It is usually prepared by a group of specialists and the content is considered company proprietary, so the distribution of this section is severely restricted. The other three main sections (or volumes) of a proposal are the executive summary, the technical section, and the management and program plan section.

Executive Summary

The executive summary, the first section of a proposal (or volume 1 of a proposal set), is part sales pitch and part proposal. It basically introduces and summarizes the proposal. Remember that proposals are read by busy people, so GET TO THE POINT! as quickly as you can. This section will be read by more people than any other section, particularly by the sponsor's management, who will not be reading the entire document. The sponsor's management will likely be the group that must review and approve the proposal evaluators' recommendations, so the executive summary requires everyone's best efforts.

Listing the strengths of your plan and of your company near the beginning helps to establish a positive mood for the entire proposal.

Show the reader why your plan deserves consideration and describe the general plan of attack, but do not include any technical details. Your readers are alert, attentive, and receptive when reading the first section of your proposal. Later they tire and their interest wanes. So make this section a clear, concise, and well-written summary.

Direct this section toward a wide readership. It should be concise, limited to about two to eight pages, and include at a minimum a summary of the organization of the proposal, a brief summary of the tasks, ideas for solving the problems, a brief résumé of your company's experience and why you are the best qualified, and a positive statement of the company's or individual's strong commitment to solving the problem. Demonstrate that you thoroughly understand the problem at issue here, and briefly describe how you've solved similar problems.

Technical Section

The technical section (or volume 2) is the heart of the proposal and should include a discussion of the problem, alternative solutions to it, and a justification for the chosen solution.

Formats for the technical discussion vary widely, depending on the sponsor's and the proposal's requirements. You may have to use a sponsor's format. If you can choose your own, a two-part format is useful for both single- and multivolume proposals:

1. *Analysis of the Problem.* Describe in detail the problem to be solved, and include a discussion of the background to convince your sponsor that you thoroughly understand the problem. Describe projects that your company and your key personnel have successfully completed that are similar to the project you're proposing and uniquely qualify you to perform the work. This section demonstrates that you have analyzed the problem thoroughly and possess the requisite knowledge, experience, management policies and procedures, personnel, and facilities to perform the job, meeting the requirements on schedule and within the budget restraints.

2. *Solution to the Problem.* Explain how your plan will be accomplished to complete the tasks you're bidding on. Your goal is to sell your ideas. This is a major part of the proposal and is the section that generally receives the most attention from the key people who will evaluate your proposal. Invest more effort on this chapter than all the other sections combined—somewhere between 50 and 70 percent of the time spent in writing the proposal. Analyze the problem, and discuss the trade-offs—the advantages and disadvantages of various po-

tential solutions. Do not rationalize your approach; prove that your recommended approach is the optimum one to solve the problem. Your goal here is to convince your potential customer that your design, analysis, and plan of attack are superior to those of all the competition.

I've accomplished trade-offs in dozens of proposals I've written. Properly conducted, they are educational, even for the writer. In some of the trade-offs, I started out believing I had the best solution (even before I had defined the problem—a poor approach). As I performed the trade-offs, comparing the advantages and disadvantages of various approaches in an unbiased manner, I often arrived at a different recommended approach. (It must have been a convincing approach to the evaluators; many of the proposals resulted in successful contract awards.) So lay aside your preconceived notions and biases when you perform trade-offs. Let the facts decide it for you.

Caution

Often a proposal becomes a confidential and proprietary communication, so you may have to limit your discussions on company proprietary matters. Proposals are supposed to be treated as confidential material by the customer, but their content can be leaked to competitors by careless or improperly motivated people.

In this or later sections, discuss other pertinent considerations, such as special designs required to meet specific environmental, safety, production, quality control, or other vital aspects of your program. This section may also cover alternative methods of solving the problems, plus any other special requirements or limitations.

One important topic concerns the exceptions and waivers one takes to the sponsor's requirements. Any waivers or exceptions to the RFP should be discussed in the technical section, along with the rationale for taking them. Taking exceptions to a sponsor's spec is hazardous to the health of your proposal because this may cause it to be declared nonresponsive and rejected. If you claim waivers or exceptions, convince the sponsor that this deviation from the specs will result in a better, and perhaps less costly and less risky, program. But be careful. The sponsors labored long and hard over their specs and may resent any attempts to rewrite or say their spec is lacking.

A proposal usually responds to a government or company pro-

curement spec. This section should analyze the specification requirements, paragraph by paragraph, using a tabular form to specify whether
you will COMPLY or NOT COMPLY with each requirement of the spec.
This is an extremely important part of a proposal because those who
evaluate the proposal often play the numbers game, counting up the
COMPLYS and DO NOT COMPLYS to compare the responses of the competitors. This is a lazy way for a potential customer to evaluate a proposal, but it happens sometimes. To avoid participating in this ill-con-
ceived numbers game, do not check the DO NOT COMPLY column. Instead,
add a column, headed REMARKS, and use it to explain and expand on
your exceptions without responding directly to the DO NOT COMPLY
handcuffs.

Management and Program Plan

This section has a number of possible parts.

▪ Management and program plan. All the management information that substantiates and justifies the claims made in the executive
summary and technical sections must be included here. The management and program plan describes how company management will supervise and provide the facilities and personnel required to perform
the program. Will a special project group be set up, for example, or
will it be company-wide participation? Use organization charts and visuals to save words and provide a clear picture of how your company
will manage the program.

▪ Applicable experience. Applicable experience describes similar
programs that you or your company has performed that pertain directly to the solution of the problem. This establishes that you are not
wandering too far afield from your specialties in performing the contract and that you have personnel skilled in the work, the ability to
manage programs of similar content, and the facilities required to perform the program.

▪ Schedules. Every proposal must perform to a schedule or it cannot be monitored and managed properly. Gantt, PERT, bar, or other
types of schedule should be included to indicate how the proposal will
be staffed and to delineate significant milestones as checkpoints along
the way to the conclusion. Schedules show staff loading and important
milestones. This section also schedules reports, products, and items to
be delivered.

These schedules will have to be updated periodically, usually in
progress reports, to assure the sponsor that the program is moving

toward its goals. There are many existing software programs that can be used to help with the mechanics of the scheduling; all of them, however, suffer from the same shortcoming: GIGO (garbage in, garbage out). All the sophisticated software in the world cannot be of any benefit if the estimates are totally incorrect.

The Precedent Sort can help remove some of this uncertainty if it is used to order and organize the sequence of tasks. It can break down large tasks into individual, manageable, and easy-to-estimate subtasks: work modules. The most important element in any cost estimating procedure is the personnel estimate. Its accuracy depends on the ability of individual estimators and their supervision. For this reason, personnel skilled in similar programs should be involved in making these important estimates.

• Personnel résumés. Résumés are an important part of a proposal (Figure 13-3). They help bolster the program's credibility by specifying the qualifications of key staff who will be working on the program and the percentage of their time they will devote to it. A standard résumé

Figure 13-3.   Typical personnel résumé.

Horatio Alger, Senior Project Manager

Education: B.S. Computer Science, University of Kentucky in Louisville, Ky. Graduate study at University of Maryland and the University of Oregon

Experience: As program manager for Project Royal, Mr. Alger supervised all programming for the satellite launch system. Prior to joining Worldwide, Alger was a system analyst for McDonnell Herman and developed software for various satellite programs, including Iliad and Odyssey. Earlier Alger supervised the design and development of the New Wave Computer, the first ternary computer, and was awarded two patents for his innovations. He also assisted in the development of ternary logic and ternary math.

Awards: Company award for best program manager 1993, 1994.

Patents: Two patents. Sole awardee for Ternary Memory, joint patent award for ternary logic circuits.

Publications: "Ternary Computers: Wave of the Future?" published in *Future Wave*, Feb. 1991.

"Managing Computer Software Development," published in *Software Design*, Jan. 1992.

format should be used for all personnel and limited to one page for each person.

▪ Company qualifications. In this section, a company résumé is required, covering the facilities available to perform the contract. Some boilerplate can be used, such as annual reports and financial statements. For this company résumé, emphasize the specific facilities that will be available for the performance of the program being bid, using photos, lists, and drawings. This section could also cover test equipment, computer systems, peripherals, floor space, office space, and any special equipment.

▪ Appendixes. The appendixes are a general catchall for specialized material that not everyone needs but that applies to the program—for example, test results, detailed discussions of theory, or mathematical proofs. Include copies of any periodical publications written by company personnel that pertain to the subject of the RFP.

Other Sections

Two other major sections should be part of every proposal: the front matter, which should consist of the cover, title page, abstract, and contents, illustrations and tables lists, and the back matter—appendixes, bibliography, and index.

The cover is the first item your reviewers see. This first impression is, in effect, your company's signature. The cover, except for very brief proposals, should be of an attractive, sturdy material that will withstand handling by many readers. It should include in clear type the title of the program, the sponsor's and proposer's names, and any special reference document number assigned or the RFP number it is responding to. Security and/or proprietary notices should also be displayed on the cover. The binding should be a spiral type or looseleaf so it can split open flat for reading. Use headings and physical dividers throughout to simplify access to the various modules. Some companies use preprinted standard covers with a centered window cut in near the top so that the information that varies from proposal to proposal can be tailored to be viewed on the title sheet behind the window. Remember that first impressions are long lasting. A quality cover can establish a good mood for the text.

The title page repeats the contents of the cover and adds other information, such as the sponsor's address, the author(s), if desired, and the submittal date of the proposal.

The abstract, contents, and illustrations and tables lists conform to the requirements already set out in Chapter 11.

Submitting the Proposal

Send a three- or four-paragraph letter of transmittal with every proposal, small and large, with the following information:

- Title and what the proposal is responding to
- Program highlights
- Contact person in case questions arise
- An expression of the proposer's commitment to performing the contract

Proposal Evaluation

The final step, evaluating your masterpiece, is now in the sponsor's hand. Proposal evaluators say that the most common reason they reject proposals is oversimplification of the requirements or the problems.

Unless you have a credible approach for solving the problem(s), your proposal will be judged nonresponsive and will be rejected. Here again is a paramount reason that a logical organization and presentation is essential to convince evaluators that you understand the problem and that your approach is solid.

Methods of evaluating proposals vary considerably, depending on the type of proposal, the cost and risk involved, and the schedule. Two systems for evaluating proposals are highlighted in the list that follows. One uses a point total of 100; the other is expressed in percentages. As you can see, the weighting factors vary widely in the first two categories, which deal with the understanding of the problem and the quality of the solution.

Evaluation Factors	*Points*	*%*
1. Understanding the requirements	30	12.5
2. Quality of proposed solution(s)	30	50
3. Management plan	10	10
4. Key personnel qualifications	20	20
5. Company capability	10	7.5
Total	100 points	100%

Appendix 13A: Commonly Used Proposal Acronyms

CBD	*Commerce Business Daily*
CDRL	*contract data requirements list*
CPFF	*cost plus fixed fee*
DOD	*Department of Defense*
FFP	*firm fixed price*
G&A	*general and administrative (expenses)*
GFE	*government-furnished equipment*
GFP	*government-furnished property*
IAW	*in accordance with*
IFB	*invitation for bid*
MIS	*management information system*
O&M	*operation and maintenance*
ODC	*other direct costs*
QC	*quality control*
R&D	*research and development*
RFP	*request for proposal*
SBA	*Small Business Administration*
SOW	*statement of work*
SSEB	*Source Selection Evaluation Board*
WBS	*work breakdown structure*

Appendix 13B: Contract Financing Methods

Firm Fixed Price (FFP). You receive a fixed amount of money for performing the contract—meeting the specs and the schedule. You receive the fixed price, whether you expend more or less than the contract specifies. Sponsors usually prefer this type of contract since they do not share the risk. Usually you have no recourse to obtain additional funding unless you can prove that the customer is demanding that you do more than the contract documents legally require. The FFP type of contract should be bid only when the tasks are precisely defined and can be cost estimated accurately.

Cost Plus Award Fee (CPAF). You receive a fee that has been negotiated between you and the customer and are rewarded with an additional variable fee that is a function of your customer's evaluation of your performance. This type of contract is desirable when you have a fairly good estimate of the tasks to be performed. It allows for more freedom in the method of performing the tasks because most costs incurred are usually reimbursed. The only gamble you take is with the size of the fee. The fee is awarded based on the sponsor's subjective evaluation of the contractor's performance, so an incentive exists to perform well and to minimize the costs incurred.

Cost Plus Fixed Fee (CPFF). A cost is negotiated between you and your customer, and you receive a fixed, previously agreed upon fee, in addition to the costs you incur. The CPFF contract is the backbone of most R&D contracts since it's difficult to estimate the amount of effort required and the eventual outcome of a research and development program.

14
Special Formats

A wide variety of additional formats is used to communicate in the business and technical professions. Each serves a specific function attuned to the unique requirements of its application. This chapter covers the following special business formats:

- Specifications
- Advertising
- Résumés
- Employee handbooks

Specifications

A specification (spec) is a formal document that describes a product or a service—equipment, a program, a procedure, or something else. The spec can describe such items as the goals of a research program, the functions equipment is to perform, or the information needed to specify and define a product or a service fully. A spec serves an important dual role as both a contractual document and a technical description.

If there is one area where innovative, creative writing ideas are desperately needed, it is in the area of eliminating the atrocious examples of writing found in specifications. Most specs are badly organized, poorly written, incomplete, and difficult, if not impossible, to understand. Yet this document serves a vital function in the business, academic, and professional worlds.

Specs can be brief and clear and adequately describe what they are supposed to specify. All it takes is a little dedicated effort to create a logical, comprehensive, well-organized, and clearly written document.

Specification writing is no different from, and requires the same care as, any other business writing.

Another factor that affects the readability and usability of specs is that often a significant portion of a spec is boilerplate, sections that are copied and used repeatedly in widely different specs without even minimum changes. In some specs, as much as 80 percent of its content is boilerplate and remains unchanged from customer to customer, as well as from one program to an entirely different program. Boilerplate serves a useful purpose in spec writing because it ensures that certain basic requirements are imposed on all procurement specs; however, when it exceeds about 30 to 40 percent of the document, the spec is in need of an extensive rewrite.

Major Classes of Specs

Two major classes of specifications will be covered in this chapter: hardware and software specifications.

A hardware specification describes a concrete object, such as a camera, a computer, or a document. It can describe such characteristics as its performance, size, shape, weight, configuration, or composition or some combination of these. A hardware spec usually specifies characteristics that can be seen, measured, and evaluated.

A software specification describes an item that is more abstract, such as a computer program, a research study, or a product evaluation program. The spec can describe such items as how a computer program functions, the goals of a research study, or the procedures and results required for an evaluation program. But software cannot be "seen" directly; it can be seen only through the secondary results of its coding.

General Writing Requirements of Specs

Regardless of type, all specs should follow the "magic three" format applicable to most writing:

- *Introduction.* Describes the purpose and the scope of the specification, plus its applicability and limitations, and lists reference specifications and documents.
- *Body.* Details the functional requirements, the performance re-

quirements, or other detailed information about the subject of the spec. The main section of the spec, it is usually titled "Requirements."

- *Conclusion.* Covers such items as inspection and testing procedures to ensure that the spec requirements are met, how the goals of a research study are to be measured, and the types of reports to be written. For a product, a conclusion includes such items as preparation for delivery, notes and data, and any appendixes.

A specification is a legal document that covers a specific product or program. When the spec details what the product or program must accomplish, *shall* and *will* are used to denote mandatory requirements. If the spec requirements provide for a choice, *should* and *may* are used.

The arabic numbering system is ideal for designating individual paragraphs or groups of paragraphs so they can be referred to by number. Paragraphs or groups of paragraphs can designated by numbers, such as:

3.1 Requirements
[Text of paragraph 3.1 is indented and begins here with one or more paragraphs.]
  3.1.1 Performance
  [Text of paragraph 3.1.1 begins here.]
    3.1.1.1 Duty cycle
    [Text of paragraph 3.1.1.1 begins here.]

Proper indentation of topics using this numbering system makes the spec easy to understand and provides a quick guide to the ordination of the topics.

The principles of good writing are especially important in specifications because topics must be clearly described in specific detail so as not to lead to false interpretations and misunderstandings. Short sentences, proper sentence construction, frequent paragraphing, minimizing jargon, using lists, and the frequent use of charts, tables, and graphs help make for a readable spec.

Hardware Specification Outline

The outline for a hardware spec presented here can be used for a wide variety of applications. Here's the outline:

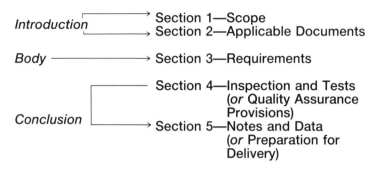

Section 1—Scope. This first part of the introduction summarizes the purpose of the spec and its applicability or limitations, and it includes a brief summary of the contents of the spec. Sometimes it specifies model numbers or versions that the spec covers, as well as any larger system it is a part of.

Section 2—Applicable Documents. Rarely can a spec completely cover the myriad of miscellaneous requirements of a specific product. This section supplies references to subsidiary and allied documents and specifications that provide details on related aspects of the product. It can contain an itemized list of documents referred to in the other sections of the spec, with their exact titles and numbers, along with a qualifying statement, such as, "These specifications are applied to the extent specified herein." For example, the main spec could delineate the overall characteristics of a medicine, what it should contain, and how it should function. This section would then refer to one or more subsidiary specs, such as "Packaging and Preservation," which would detail how that medicine (and all similar medicines) should be packaged and stored, shelf life, methods of handling, and other pertinent data.

Section 2 should also list other standards (e.g., company, industry, or government) and publications that apply to the product being described.

Section 3—Requirements. The body describes the basic requirements of the product. It includes such items as product performance, design, program goals, testing procedures, and configuration. This is the longest and most detailed section—the heart of the spec. It is tailored to the specific requirements of the hardware. This section can detail the content, color, shape, size, and, most important, the performance requirements of the product. At least 60 to 80 percent of the effort spent on preparing a spec should be expended on this section.

Section 4—Inspection and Tests [or Quality Assurance Provisions]. This part of the conclusion lists the tests and inspections that must be performed to ensure that the product meets the requirements of Section 3 of the spec and the applicable specs listed in Section 2. This includes such items as performance requirements, safety, reliability, and shelf-life.

Section 5—Notes and Data [or Preparation for Delivery]. This catch-all section contains information of a general nature that doesn't logically fit anywhere else in the spec—for example, a glossary to define terms used in the spec or requirements for shipping, storage, and handling.

The Appendix can include large (multipage) data, tables, or general information whose bulk is too great to include in the main body of the spec.

Software Specification Outline

A software specification covers more abstract items that cannot be observed directly, such as a software program or a research study, but whose results can be measured or observed.

The general outline for a software specification presented here is adapted from the requirements of the *IEEE Guide to Software Requirements Specification,* ANSI/IEEE Std 830–1984:

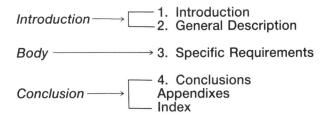

1.0 *Introduction.* This first section states the purpose of the spec and the intended audience. The scope identifies the software product by title and version, or the study by name, and defines the general goals the software product is required to accomplish or the goals of the study. The introduction contains a list of reference specs that are imposed and lists each document by title, number, date, and publisher, as well as where the references may be obtained. Finally, it summarizes the contents of the remainder of the spec.

2.0 General Description. For a software program, this section describes the general factors that affect the product and its requirements, puts the software product in perspective (is it self-contained or a portion of a larger system?), and defines the principal interfaces, as well as the computer hardware and peripheral equipment it is to function with.

For a research study, this section describes the general factors that affect the performance of the study—whether it is a self-contained study or depends on the results of other related research studies—and any specific inputs or data from other sources that are required.

For a software spec, a summary of the functions the software is to perform follows, plus the general characteristics of the users of the product that will affect the requirements. Tables, charts, and visuals define these characteristics. This section also examines the general constraints that limit the developer's options for designing the system, such as interfaces, hardware limitations, safety, and security.

Similarly, for a research study spec, the goals of the study are delineated, along with the constraints (budget, time, personnel) that affect attainment of these goals.

3.0 Specific Requirements. The body of the spec covers the details the software developer or study personnel need so they can create and design the program. Write it so that it does not restrict the design to using specific hardware or techniques or does not place specific restrictions on approaches for a study. Place emphasis on the results, not the method of obtaining them. Specify how inputs to the software are transformed into outputs, the fundamental functions of the software.

For a study, call out the methods by which the input data will help attain the goals, and describe in detail the inputs and outputs, including sources, how they're measured, quantity, type, timing, range, and operator action. Desired responses to abnormal situations should also be covered for both the software program and the research study. Specify the performance requirements or results in such a manner that they may be tested and measured for both software and the study.

4.0 Conclusions. This section covers the test methods—the quality control for ensuring that the software meets the spec requirements and that the study attains its goals. It and any subsequent sections can also detail how the software will be delivered and the accompanying documentation or final report for the study. If you have used a lot of acronyms and new terms in the specs, they should be repeated in a glossary.

Advertising

Most advertising can be created using the basic Four Part Formula: HEY! YOU! SEE? SO! Although formats differ in various media ranging from brochures to product bulletins, the same basic principles apply to all. Advertising media can range from a single sheet of black-and-white test to multicolored, multipaged documents. The goal of advertising is to communicate the essentials of a product or service quickly and effectively to potential customers to convince them to buy the product or service. Here are some recommendations for achieving this goal:

- *Use a headline—a* HEY! YOU!—*at the top,* preferably a short, bold, large-print headline to grab readers' attention and convey the most important information at a glance. Leave white space above and below the headline so it will stand out, and use upper- and lowercase to make the headline easy to read. Smaller print and bold subheadings can be added to elaborate on the headline. Color considerably enhances the overall appearance and attractiveness of all material. Remember to bring the YOU! into the headline or the subheading, either directly or implied.

- *Pull the* YOU! *the buyer, in even more strongly in the first paragraph.* Your text must have a strong, concise, selling message, or your customers will read no further. Use a variety of methods—photographs, charts, tables—to present the maximum amount of information in the minimum space.

- *Be sure the body, the* SEE?*, is complete and answers all major questions.* Develop hard-hitting reasons for buying your product in a logical sequence organized with the Precedent Sort. Offer convincing proof that the customer needs your product. Use frequent paragraphing and short, succinct, easy-to-read sections.

- *Conclude with a call to action, the* SO!*, that is precise, clear, and definite.* Everything you have written before this section is directed toward one object: persuading readers to act. Make it easy for them by answering the key questions: How can they buy your product? Who is selling it? How much does it cost? Where can they buy it?

Résumés

One of the most important documents you'll ever write is your personal résumé (Figure 14-1). A well-written résumé is a passport, a letter

Figure 14-1. Another typical personnel résumé.

Horatio Alger	Married
2435 Maine Street	Excellent health
Watkins, Oreg. 97741	Willing to relocate
Telephone (505) 746-6875	

EMPLOYMENT OBJECTIVE: Management of major software program

Education
Graduate study in advanced computer technology at University of Illinois, 1987, and University of Oregon 1994-95. B.S. in Computer Science, Telecomm major, University of Kentucky, Louisville, Ky., 1987.

Experience
7/94–   Rocket Production Systems, Springfield, Oreg. *Program manager* for Project Royal. Supervised all programming for satellite launch system. Developed program code for automated launch for NASA 345 computer, supervised team of 22 senior programmers.

2/92–7/94   McDonnell Herman Aeronautics, Kankakee, Ill. *Senior system analyst.* Developed software for various satellite programs, including Iliad and Odyssey. Also responsible for design and development of New Wave Computer, history's first ternary computer now being used by McDonnell. Awarded two patents for these innovations. Assisted in development of ternary logic and ternary math for New Wave computer.

Awards
Rocket Productions Company award for best program manager 1994.

Patents
Two patents. Sole awardee for Ternary Memory, joint patent award for ternary logic circuits.

Publications
"Ternary Computers: Wave of the Future?" published in *Future Wave,* Feb. 1991.
"Managing Computer Software Development," published in *Software Design,* Jan. 1992.
Personal references available on request.

of introduction, a key to open doors to new opportunities that may otherwise be closed to you. It should:

- Detail the work you've done and any special achievements or awards you've received.
- List schools and jobs in inverse chronological order.
- Be customized to match the requirements of the specific position you're applying for. Don't use the same résumé to apply for a job as a personnel manager and for a training manager.
- Contain highly specific data stated tersely in phrases rather than in complete statements
- Be error free, clear, neat, and easy to read.
- Be single spaced and use one or two pages at the most.

The format used in Figure 14-1 places the employment dates in the left column. Résumés may be arranged in other formats using job titles, companies, or education as the left column entry, depending on which you feel is the most important to emphasize.

A natural marriage between the PC and on-line data banks has provided a new method of conducting a job search. Some college students can now connect into a network having nationwide employment ads that specify necessary qualifications and salary ranges. Students can transmit their résumés and then reply to prescreening questions, all from the comfort and convenience of a home or college PC. This eliminates waiting in line, sign-up sheets, travel, and most interviewing delays. A natural and likely evolution of this service would be to extend it to all professionals seeking employment.

Job searches, however, should not be limited to responding only to advertised openings. Studies have shown that fewer than one in every four job openings is advertised. Unsolicited applications to numerous companies can open the door to these unadvertised job openings.

Employee Handbooks

An employee handbook serves a dual purpose: introducing new employees to a company's rules and regulations and serving as the document that details a company's policies for its employees. A number of techniques can make this important document easy to read and understand.

A friendly, positive approach is necessary to establish the proper relationship between the company and its employees. For example, instead of prescribing "smoking regulations," the emphasis on the topic can be reversed and covered as "smoking privileges" to inform the employees where smoking is permitted, not forbidden. Also, instead of using an unpalatable term such as "grievance procedure," the more positive "suggestion procedure" can be documented.

Another technique that imparts information in an easy-to-understand and nondogmatic manner is the use of a question-and-answer format, much like that occurring in a conversation between the employee and company management—for example:

Question: What are the normal working hours?
Answer: Normal working hours are from 8 A.M. until 5 P.M., with one hour off for lunch. Lunch hour is noon to 1 P.M.; however, some lunch hours may be staggered as determined by mutual agreement between you and your supervisor.

Another technique that saves words and increases understanding is the judicious application of tables, charts, and cartoons to explain procedures. For example, a hospitalization plan's benefits and charges can be best explained with charts, tables, and specific examples rather than only straight text.

A handbook typically has two major divisions: "Our Organization—How It Works" and "Employee Benefits—What We Do for You."

The first section, dealing with company organization, should use brief, simple, organization charts to introduce the company and to illustrate how each employee fits into the overall picture. Titles should be used instead of names on the chart since personnel changes quickly outdate printed versions. The specific functions of the various departments should be illustrated, again using functional names on a chart, rather than text, as much as possible.

The section dealing with employee benefits could list and describe some of the following topics:

- Attendance
- Health and Safety
- Hospitalization Plan
- Leave of Absence
- Life Insurance
- Overtime
- Pay Period

- Performance Evaluation
- Profit Sharing
- Promotion Policy
- Retirement Plan
- Sick Leave
- Smoking Privileges
- Suggestions
- Training
- Tuition Reimbursement
- Vacations

Use an alphabetical order of listing, and include a good contents list and an index to help locate material. Each description should be reasonably self-sufficient so that employees need not search back and forth to find a complete answer. The question-and-answer approach is ideally suited to this section.

15

The Book

When you're ready for that ultimate challenge in business writing, the book, this chapter will guide you on this fascinating journey.

When you consider that writing a book is roughly equivalent to writing ten to fifteen articles, the task is not so intimidating. By writing one article a month, you can complete an entire book in a little more than a year. If you have enough knowledge about or can do in-depth research on a viable subject, then you're ready to consider writing a book.

Embarking on the Journey

There are many compelling reasons for writing a book:

- It is one of the most prestigious and satisfying achievements a business or professional person can accomplish.
- You are the only person in the world who possesses your knowledge. You can profit in many ways from your unique knowledge if it is properly organized and written.
- You owe it to your colleagues to make a permanent contribution to the literature of your profession.
- The market is excellent, and you'll earn money for your efforts.

First, determine whether there is a market for a new book. If any of the following factors is true, a new book is needed:

- No existing book covers your subject, which is big enough for a book.

- The books available on the subject are outdated, and enough advances have been made in the field to fill a new book.
- You have something unique to offer—enough to fill an entire book.

Finally, can you write an entire book? The magnitude of the task may seem daunting, but consider this: An average nonfiction book is made up of around 200 typeset pages, or about 400 double-spaced typed pages. You need to write only 8 double-spaced pages a week to complete a book in a year.

Before you embark on this fascinating journey, answer these questions:

- Does a market exist for your subject?
- How large is the potential market?
- Do you have, or can you obtain, a thorough knowledge of your subject? Do you have a strong desire to inform others about your subject?
- What books already published will compete with your book?
- What can you offer that is unique enough to make yours a better book than those of your competitors?
- Do you have a strong sense of organization and the ability to envision, design, and complete a major project in an effective and logical manner?
- Will your subject still be current a few years from now? Remember that it takes from twelve months to two years or more from the time you begin writing until your book is published.
- Can you handle constructive as well as destructive criticism? Constructive criticism should be evaluated carefully to determine how it can help you in the future. Destructive criticism is written by people who envy your accomplishment.
- Do you have the drive to persist in your project for the six months to two years it will take you to write your book?

Step-by-Step Procedure

Writing a book is a four-phase process:

1. The *preproposal phase* is required to prepare to write a proposal to obtain a contract to write a book. It covers the exploratory

research needed to choose a subject, title, and purpose for your book and to determine if a market exists.

2. The *proposal phase* is the most crucial of the four. Most nonfiction books are sold on the basis of a proposal that contains a detailed outline and one or more sample chapters. Until you are established as a credible author, the proposal phase will probably be the most difficult.

3. For the *contract phase,* you sign a contract and write your book that follows the outline and sample chapter(s) you submitted with your proposal. This is the longest phase and where your real work is accomplished. Your contract will probably specify that your book should contain a specific number of words or pages and a given number of illustrations and should be delivered as a completed manuscript, conforming to a specific format, by a specified date—typically within six to twelve months.

4. During the *postcontract phase* you review galley proofs, help promote the sale of your soon-to-be-published book, and start planning your next one.

Preproposal Phase

The step-by-step procedure for the preproposal phase of writing a book is diagramed in Figure 15-1.

Selecting a Subject, Title, and Purpose

An idea for a book usually develops over a long period of time. As you read related works, discuss subjects with colleagues, and become aware of the lack of up-to-date information on your subject, begin to consider your subject in depth. Define a purpose and perhaps even create a working title for your book.

The selection of a subject, or a title, or a purpose is interrelated. You may start out with one of these and then fill in the others later, or you may simply create one of the three, and the others will naturally develop from your research and writing.

You may decide you want to write a book for the business market and choose a subject to interest this specific market. Later you may broaden your title and/or purpose that extends this market to many related professions, such as engineering and medicine. Or perhaps you have a definite purpose in mind, such as writing a book that teaches people how to use a spreadsheet for a specific type of business appli-

Figure 15-1. Preproposal phase for a book.

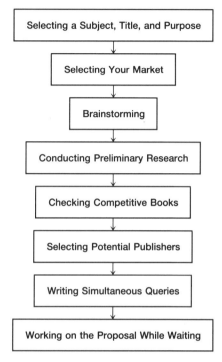

cation. This is enough to get you started, but you have to expand the examples to cover a wide range of spreadsheet applications to fill an entire book. The subject is implied; the title can come later.

As long as you can choose one of these three, you have made a positive start.

Selecting Your Market

Consider the market you will aim the book at. The market potential of a book is uppermost in the minds of the editors you are going to query, so this step requires considerable preliminary research. The market should be as broad as possible, yet if it becomes too general, it may lose some of its uniqueness.

Publishers of professional books want to be fairly sure they can sell at least 5,000 to 7,500 copies of a book they have invested in. If you're writing for a specific audience, such as all the mechanical engineers in the United States, you can probably find the number of mechanical engineers listed in *Statistical Abstracts*. If you write an excellent book, it's possible to reach from 5 to 10 percent of the potential audience in three to five years of sales, so you can estimate your potential market on this basis.

But some markets are difficult to define. If you're writing a book on a general word processing program, you'll have trouble establishing concrete numbers for your potential market since it may include scientists, business professionals, secretaries, and stock clerks. If you can locate a similar book that has already been published and obtain information on its sales, you may get some idea of the potential market. Otherwise you have to make your best educated guess and justify it by some related statistics.

Don't forget the enormous potential of the international market. Books on computers, management, and electronics sell well in the international market since these subjects are universal in their application. In contrast, some engineering books, because of wide variations in engineering and building codes and because they are based on the English system of measurement, do not sell well in the international market. Neither do books on law and accounting because they're based on U.S. laws and procedures.

One important positive factor in writing for the professional market is that professionals don't mind paying a high price for books. Professionals are a relatively affluent, book-buying market who must invest in the latest work to keep pace with the rapid and often radical developments in their professions.

If you're also aiming for the high school and college textbook market and your text is not quickly outdated, it can be sold for as long as ten to twenty years after initial publication, an excellent long-term market.

Brainstorming

Depending on your subject, the amount of brainstorming you need to accomplish can vary considerably. If you're already an expert on your subject, you need only brainstorm enough to come up with some form for your material. But if you've selected a subject that you know very little about, you need to flex your creativity muscles and concentrate on your subject, title, and purpose. Perhaps all you'll end up with after a brainstorming session is a number of questions. This is fine. You're probably going to ask yourself the same questions your reader will ask, so this gives you an excellent basis for your preliminary research. Actually, some of the best nonfiction books have been written by authors not skilled in the topic of the book, but motivated to thoroughly re-search the subject. The reason for the success of this approach is that the author starts from the same place as the reader and is able to ask the same questions the beginner does, and then answer those questions.

Remember that many so-called new ideas are nothing more than a combination or fusion of old ideas. Often a new slant on an old idea, an unusual combination of existing ideas, or a new arrangement of old ideas can qualify as a new idea. Henry Ford's automobile wasn't a new idea but the clever combination of the combustion engine and a horse-drawn buggy.

If your knowledge of your subject is sparse, try asking What, Why, Who, When, Where, and How. Get a set of six 3- by 5-inch cards, and write one of these words at the top of each card. Spread the cards out in front of you, pick up any card at random, and use the word to phrase a question about your subject. "Why should I write about program management?" "What audience should I write for?" Write the questions down on the card. Probably by the time you've written the first question, another will pop into your mind. "What types of programs should I cover?" "How often should program reviews be held?" "What are some techniques to make meetings more efficient?" Write all of them down on the appropriate card and continue until you run dry.

Conducting Preliminary Research

With the questions, statements, and/or facts you created in your brainstorming session, get ready to find answers to the questions, to verify and expand on the facts, and to sharpen the focus of your book. You also need to reassure yourself that you can obtain enough information to write an entire book. (Chapter 7 described the procedures and sources for this step.)

By the time you've completed your preliminary research, you should have enough topics and an adequate supply of supplementary material to form a skeleton of your book and to be able to write a brief text summary (about a half to one page per chapter) of all the chapters. This information is needed for your query letter and your book proposal.

Conduct your preliminary research in enough depth so that you have at least twice as many topics and twice as much material as you'll need for your book proposal. You want to be able to select and build around the best of the best.

Checking Competitive Books

Once you have completed enough preliminary research to feel confident about the subject, check the competition. Your quickest and easiest sources are the local library and bookstores. Locate books on similar subjects that you can review to determine how different, or how outdated, or how lacking in detail they are compared to your proposed book.

Two other excellent sources are *Books in Print* (*BIP*), a multivolume series listing all the books currently being published in the United States, and *Forthcoming Books*, which lists the books to be published in the next five months by trade publishers. *BIP* has one set of volumes arranged alphabetically by author, a second set by title, and the third set by subject. Unfortunately, these references list only the title, author, publisher, and cost; they provide no information about the books' contents. You'll have to go to other sources to check this further. Photocopy the applicable pages, and use them to check your competition further.

Using these sources, identify the competitive books and check them out of the library or obtain them on interlibrary loan, purchase them, or check periodical indexes and book review indexes to see if the books have been reviewed in periodicals.

When you review the competition, be sure to notice the publication date, the size of the book, the number of illustrations, the cost of the book, and the publisher, and review in detail the contents of the book. You'll need all of this information for use in your query letter to convince your editor that you've done your homework and that your proposed book is superior to all the competition.

Other sources to check for competitive books are:

- *Book Review Digest,* issued monthly and with annual accumulations. Selected reviews from general magazines are given in digest form. Both pro and con reviews are given and include exact citations of the original review.
- *Book Review Index,* which is more inclusive than the *Book Review Digest* but does not offer digests of the reviews. It specifies where and when a book was reviewed so you can locate the review in the appropriate periodical issue.
- *Paperbound Books in Print,* a semiannually published reference that lists by author, title, and subject the in-print paperbacks, mainly for U.S. publishers.

- The library, to determine which publishers publish books similar in content to your proposed book. If you find publishers that do, and if your subject is sufficiently different or much more up to date than their published books, they may be receptive to a query for an updated version of the subject.

Selecting Potential Publishers

Literary Market Place lists over 1,700 publishers. Small publishers produce from 10 to perhaps 30 titles each year. Large publishers may publish from 50 to 200 or more titles in a year. Other references that list publishers, along with the types of books they publish, are *The Writer's Market, The Writer's Handbook,* and the principal writing magazines, *Writer* and *Writer's Digest,* all probably available in your local library.

The choice of a small versus a large publisher is an individual one. Large publishers are more prestigious, have larger and more specialized sales forces, employ people who are more skilled in the specialized arts of the publishing profession, and usually have a larger sales distribution network. You can probably obtain a bigger cash advance from a large publisher, too. However, this bigness can lead to making you feel that your book is just one product in an assembly line—one of the hundreds they publish each year. Since the success or failure of a single book will not make or break a big company, a large publisher may not devote what you think are adequate resources to promoting your book. Moreover, it will probably take a longer time to publish your book—often as much as a year or longer after you submit a completed manuscript.

Small publishers can give you much more personal attention and make you feel as if your book is an important one in their small catalog of perhaps twenty to fifty books. Because the success of a small publisher depends on the collective success of a limited number of books, it is highly motivated to promote each book as vigorously as possible. And if you can find the right publisher, you're more likely to be satisfied with the results of the promotional campaigns. Also, a small publisher can move faster and publish your book as quickly as six months after you submit your completed manuscript.

Don't deal with vanity or subsidy publishers. *You* have to pay *them* to publish your book, and they can waste thousands of your hard-earned dollars. The sales of such books are minimal; you have to sell them yourself.

Writing Simultaneous Queries

When you compose a query letter (Figure 15-2), prepare about twenty-five simultaneous submissions. After all, your query is only a sales letter from you offering each publisher an opportunity to review your book proposal. You want to sample a large market for possible interest in your book. I recommend a large number of simultaneous submis-

Figure 15-2. Sample query letter for a book.

April 5, 1992

Mr. Alan J. Allan, Acquisitions Editor
Business Publications, Inc.
P.O. Box 999
New York, N.Y. 10020

Dear Mr. Allan,

Much day—to—day business is transacted in writing,
so all business professionals must learn how to put their
ideas into writing. In some limited respects, personal
computers have simplified business writing. Word pro—
cessing programs, electronic thesauruses, spelling
checkers, and computerized grammarians take much of the
drudgery out of writing, automating what were once
fairly onerous tasks.
In spite of these advances in automation, one basic
aspect of business writing has been sorely neglected:
the vital work that must be accomplished before one be—
gins to write. This includes brainstorming, research—
ing, and organizing the material that forms the basis of
all business writing. To fill this lack, I've developed,
after many years of experimentation, a new writing con—
cept that uses techniques developed for and that com—
plement the personal computer. This new concept I call
"modular writing" breaks down a writing project of any
degree of complexity into easy—to—write, self—suffi—
cient modules.

An important key to modular writing is the "Precedent Sort," an organizing technique I adapted from the "bubble-sort" of computer programming. The Precedent Sort is an easy-to-use method for ordering all the material for a writing project.

My book, *Business Writing the Modular Way*, describes this new and revolutionary technique. I also cover many other related business writing topics including: How to Take Notes, Using On-line Databases, Brainstorming, Library and Document Research, Ordering Methods, Building an Article/Report, Building a Book, Word Processing Secrets for Business Writing . . . plus much, much more.

This book is directed to all business professionals. No competitive book covers the basic topics of modular writing and the Precedent Sort. The application of these techniques to writing is unique with myself.

Over 2 million business professionals can profit from this book. A mere 5 percent penetration of this potential readership would yield a market of 100,000 copies. I'm also including exercises at the end of each chapter so the book can be used as a college text.

I've had seven nonfiction books and a number of articles published in national periodicals. A degreed engineer, I've worked on and managed a wide variety of engineeering projects and have written for over twenty years. I managed a writing department for five years and served as an editor for two periodicals. I've also had extensive experience in computer programming. The diverse professions of writing and computer programming have much in common, as you will see from my proposal.

Would you like to see a detailed outline, plus two completed chapters to review? I've enclosed an SASE. Thanks.

Sincerely,

Harley Bjelland

Harley Bjelland
P.O. Box 1111
North City, Oreg. 97499
(503) 777-5532

sions because it's difficult to determine ahead of time the precise topics in which a specific publisher is interested. Moreover, often a publisher will take anywhere from a week or two to many months to respond to your query. If you address only one publisher at a time, it could take years to receive a positive response. And sad to say, some publishers don't even bother to respond to a query, even when you supply a self-addressed, stamped envelope (SASE). It's also a good boost for your self-confidence to receive more than one positive response to your query.

When you write your query, address it to the acquisitions editor, an editor that covers the field of your interest, or the editor-in-chief. Address the editor by name and title. Send an SASE.

Your query must speak to the vital question that is uppermost in most editors' minds: "What is the potential market?" You should have some idea of the potential market, not only in the proposed audience but also the number of copies you think can be sold. In your query, give the potential publisher your marketing ideas. Hand address your envelopes; a printed label makes your letter look too much like junk mail. Send follow-up letters in two months if you haven't received a reply.

Working on Your Proposal While Waiting

Continue to research your subject while you wait for a response from your publishers. Ideally, if you have an outline and one sample chapter drafted by the time you receive one or more replies to your query, you'll be able to speed up the approval process. Don't put your outline and sample chapter(s) into final form until you receive a positive reply from one or more editors since they may suggest some revisions of your outline, changing the slant or the scope of your proposed book.

Proposal Phase

Within two to three weeks after you mail your query letters, you should receive replies. The responses may be one of the following types:

1. We are interested in seeing your outline and sample chapters.
2. Your outline sounds interesting, but could you slant it a little more toward the college student as well as the professional to widen the sales potential? If you can, send us a revised outline and your sample chapters.

3. Sorry, but this subject is out of our field of expertise [*or* we recently published a book on this subject].
4. No response. Unfortunately this happens frequently, even though all an editor has to do is to scribble a note on your query and say "not interested." They can use your SASE to reply, but some do not even bother. It's not unusual to receive ten to twenty rejections before your proposal is accepted, so don't be discouraged. Persist.

Persistence is probably as important as talent in finding the right publisher. In my opinion, getting a book published is about one-fourth subject, one-fourth persistence, one-fourth talent, and one-fourth luck and good timing. Even great writers have a difficult time getting started.

Zane Grey, one of the most prolific writes of modern times, had many disappointments before his work was accepted. An unsuccessful dentist, he had decided to take up writing. He sent his hundredth attempt, a long book, to a publishing house and never had a reply.

One day he was in New York and decided to see about his manuscript.

"You've wasted enough of our time with your junk," the publisher shouted at him. "Why don't you go back to pulling teeth? You can't write, you never could write, and you never will be able to write!"

But Grey was persistent and sent the book to still another publisher, who thought the subject was interesting and timely and bought it immediately. The name of the book was *Riders of the Purple Sage*. It sold over a million copies.

The subject Grey chose, his persistence, talent, luck, and good timing paid off handsomely.

Assuming you receive a letter of interest from one or more publishers, you are ready for the most important phase of all: the proposal phase (Figure 15-3).

Top-Down Design of Chapters

The procedure for the top-down design of chapters was thoroughly covered in Chapter 8, although a few extra suggestions apply specifically to books.

Save each chapter in a separate file on your memory disk. Give each chapter a specific and unique designation and number so you can locate it easily. If you try to work with a number of chapters as a single document, all the writing and editing processes are slowed down

Figure 15-3. Proposal phase for a book.

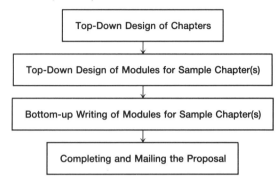

drastically. Also you need a fairly good idea about the contents of each chapter so you can write a short summary of each.

Figure 15-4 illustrates the step-by-step, top-down design procedure for chapters. Most of the steps have been covered in earlier chapters and will not be repeated here; however, a few comments will be added to clarify these steps specifically for designing and writing books.

Figure 15-4. Procedure for the top-down design of chapters.

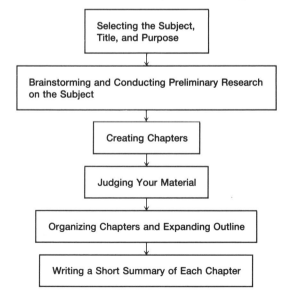

Selecting the Subject, Title, and Purpose

Select your subject and purpose with great care since you must live with them for six months to a year or longer. Although the title can be changed easily and does not become important until it becomes a sales tool when you submit your proposal, the subject and purpose are two fixed items that you cannot change without starting all over again, so choose them only after much study, deliberation, and research.

Because of the long time interval from starting a book to publication and marketing of it, your subject must be capable of living for five years or more. Don't waste time writing about a current fad. By the time your book is published, the fad could be as out-of-date as the hula hoop.

Your purpose defines why you are writing the book and who you are writing it for. Usually the purpose for business writing is to inform and/or convince. You also must choose your audience. Will you be addressing all the business professionals in the United States? Will your book address college students as well? Will it be useful for stock clerks and secretaries or only company executives? Keep your potential audience in mind at all times when you conduct research, develop the outline, and write the book. This isn't a decision you can change when you are halfway through the project. It's a fundamental decision that must be made at the beginning and maintained throughout.

Brainstorming and Conducting Preliminary Research on the Subject

The basic processes of brainstorming and preliminary research have already been covered. When they are applied to designing an entire book, the magnitude of the task expands.

You will have to accomplish considerably more brainstorming and research on your subject because a book will encompass many aspects and in-depth concentration. You can't, for example, write only about the limited application of a spreadsheet procedure for making personnel estimates. You must also include procedures for calculating manufacturing costs and quantity discounts, for pricing options to your standard product line, for computing cost escalation due to rising labor and material costs, and a host of other related applications.

You need to review a large number of references and obtain information from a wide variety of authors. Review both old and new publications about your subject. Broaden the scope as much as possible—not only to fill your book but also to attract a wide readership. Think big.

Creating Chapters

Chapters form the basic skeleton of a book. Each chapter should be roughly equal in length and importance of the topic addressed in it. For example, you can't devote one chapter to such a complex subject as production planning and another on such a small subject as how to fill out and file purchase orders.

The list of chapter titles should provide an overall summary of the book's contents and the depth of coverage. Chapter titles should follow each other in some logical order (order of increasing importance, for example, or general to specific), and there shouldn't be any unnecessary or missing topics. This list need only be a tentative assignment that you can change as you research and design. I do considerable rearrangement—expanding, combining, separating, and renumbering chapters, often as late as approaching the final drafts of a book, an easy task with a word processor.

Judging Your Material

At this stage of design, don't judge your material too critically. Eliminate or combine obvious duplications and any items that are far afield from your subject, but hold on to all material that you are not certain of; you may find a home for it later. Err on the side of having too much information rather than too little. You have a few hundred pages to fill.

Organizing Chapters and Expanding the Outline

Use the Precedent Sort to organize the chapters in one of the logical orders described in Chapter 2. Assign sequential numbers to the chapters and a short title for each, and use this reference as the basis for your outline.

Then sort the remaining material from your brainstorming and preliminary research sessions into the proper chapters. Order the material using the Precedent Sort, and expand your outline. List all the subordinate material under each chapter title, and add it to flesh out your outline. You will then have a solid basis for writing a short description of the content of each chapter.

Writing a Short Summary of Each Chapter

Using the information from your outline, expand it into a short text summary of each chapter (about a half to a full page for each). Use the present tense ("Chapter 1 describes the techniques of organizing a development project . . ."). These summaries will form key parts of your book proposal. The chapter numbers and content may change later if your publisher makes suggestions or if you have some second thoughts as to how many chapters to use and what they should contain.

Top-Down Design of Modules for Sample Chapter(s)

The steps for top-down design of a sample chapter are outlined in Figure 15-5. Each chapter is first brainstormed and researched and then broken down into modules. The content of the individual modules is then judged, and the modules are organized and used to update the sample chapter outline.

Most of these steps have also been covered previously and will not

Figure 15-5. Procedure for the top-down design of sample chapter(s).

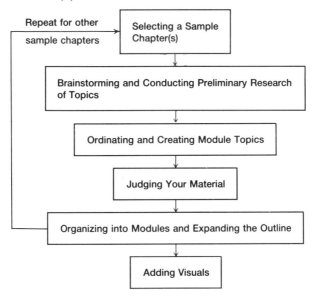

be repeated here. However, some of the steps will be expanded as they specifically apply to designing and writing a book.

Selecting Sample Chapter(s)

Probably the best choices to use as sample chapters are Chapters 1 and 2. Chapter 1 introduces the subject and summarizes the rest of the book. Design and write it largely by converting the modules in your detailed outline to text. In Chapter 2, introduce some special aspect of your subject to demonstrate your in-depth knowledge of it and your ability to write clearly, concisely, and authoritatively. If, however, you have something especially noteworthy to say in a different chapter, use it as your second sample chapter.

Brainstorming and Conducting Preliminary Research of Topics

Brainstorm and conduct preliminary research to accumulate enough material for filling the chapter. Expand the subject of your book using the techniques described in Chapter 8. You may end up only with questions after brainstorming, but they can form a solid basis for preliminary research.

Research a number of diverse references from different authors so you achieve a varied set of views on your subject. You have to prove to the publisher that you can cover your subject thoroughly, accurately, and objectively.

Ordinating and Creating Module Topics

Use the techniques described in Chapter 8 to ordinate your material to create module topics—from ten to twenty or more modules per chapter. Modules, much like chapters, should cover topics of roughly equal importance, although the length of each can vary considerably (as you will note from this chapter). Some modules will contain only a paragraph; longer modules may require several pages.

Judging Your Material

Don't judge your material too harshly. Basically eliminate duplications and combine similar topics. The more thorough judging can come when you write the sample chapters.

Organizing into Modules and Expanding the Outline

Use the Precedent Sort to organize the modules in one of the orders listed in Chapter 2. The module-to-module order used can be different from that used for chapter to chapter, although the same order should be used throughout a given chapter. Add this new information to your outline.

Adding Visuals

Add the visuals for this sample chapter to the outline so they form an integral part of the chapter. The visuals need not be finalized yet; sketches or even notes about them are adequate as long as they are completely defined. If adding visuals necessitates creating more modules, do this work now.

Many potential sources exist for visuals—both your own company, which will view them as good advertising, and outside companies, which may be eager to supply free illustrations of their products as long as they are given credit.

My own preference is to create as many of the visuals as possible with a word processor or with special computer graphic programs. In this way I get precisely what I want instead of having to settle for another company's idea of what they think I need. Sophisticated computer graphic programs can produce complex and varied visuals. Make full use of this capability.

Another potential source is the clip art folders that are available in some public libraries and art stores and as computer clip art. These visuals are usually free.

Repeat these procedures for any other sample chapters you plan to use in your proposal, and update your outline.

Bottom-Up Writing of Modules for Sample Chapter(s)

Figure 15-6 outlines the procedures for writing the text for the sample chapter(s) for your proposal. Because all of these steps have been thoroughly covered already, I offer only a few suggestions here:

• When you write and revise the module text, remember that this material will serve as your sales proposal, so the text must be your best

Figure 15-6. Procedure for writing a sample chapter.

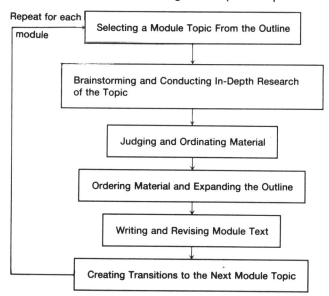

writing. Use all the word processing tools at your disposal—including the speller, the thesaurus, and the grammar checker.

- Write a series of complete modules for one chapter. Then, after you have completed most of the modules for it, review and revise the entire chapter, recheck the transitions, and update your outline if it has changed during the writing process.

- Complete any other sample chapter(s) you have scheduled. And when you have completed them, review and revise them once again.

Completing and Mailing the Proposal

You should now have the basis for your proposal:

1. A comprehensive outline with a one-half to a full-page summary of each chapter.
2. One or two completed sample chapters
3. A cover letter.
4. Finished visuals for the sample chapters.

You should be able to estimate the total number of double-spaced manuscript pages and the quantity and types (photographs, line drawings, computer graphics) of illustrations, information your editor uses to calculate the cost of producing the book and the number of copies that must be sold to make a profit. If your book doesn't promise to make a profit, it will probably be rejected.

Your cover letter should have both your mailing address and telephone number so the editor can contact you easily.

Send your proposal in a sturdy hand-addressed envelope, and mail it first class. Enclose a large envelope with adequate postage for a return trip (which you hope won't be needed). If you don't include return postage and a return envelope, you may never see those copies again.

Contract Phase

The exciting day has arrived: A publisher has called and decided to publish your book. He or she will send you a contract to review and sign and style sheets with instructions on how to prepare the manuscript. Figure 15-7 outlines the happy steps of this phase.

Figure 15-7. Contract phase for a book.

How About an Agent?

Most agents charge 10 percent of the author's royalty income, and some charge as much as 15 to 20 percent. They also charge for incidental expenses, such as reproduction costs and postal and telephone charges. The agent takes those expenses out of your income or bills you for them.

Unless you have a real blockbuster of a book, it's unlikely you will be able to interest an agent in representing you. Few agents handle business and technical books, so you'll have trouble even locating one. On the other hand, you probably don't need an agent. Publishers of professional books usually make their decisions based on the subject, the author's credentials, and the market potential. Also publishing contracts for professional books are fairly standard, so it's unlikely that any agent can significantly improve the terms.

If you still feel you would like to try to interest an agent to represent you, over three hundred agents or agencies are listed in the *Literary Market Place*. This listing describes the agents' specialties, the professional organizations they belong to, and whether they read unsolicited queries or manuscripts, and indicates whether they are interested in representing new authors.

Do not deal with any so-called agents who charge reading fees or evaluation fees. They make their money in this manner, not through sales of books, as they should. An agent should not receive any money until your book is sold.

Negotiating

Many of the contracts for business books are fairly standard, and there is not much room for negotiation. A number of books have been written on this subject, so refer to some of these if you have detailed questions about a contract.

- *The Writer's Legal Guide*, by Tad Crawford (New York: Hawthorn Books, 1978)
- *How to Get Your Book Published*, by Herbert W. Bell (Cincinnati: Writer's Digest Books, 1985)
- *How to Understand and Negotiate a Book Contract or Magazine Agreement*, by Richard Balkin (Cincinnati: Writer's Digest Books, 1985)

The following observations may help you when negotiating your contract:

- Try to get the book copyrighted in your name rather than in the publisher's. This gives you more freedom to use the material again in your future books.
- You'll probably be able to obtain an advance of about $2,000 to $5,000 for a technical book—half on signing your contract and half upon delivery of a satisfactory manuscript.
- A publisher usually gives you about ten free copies of your book on publication. You can purchase additional copies at a discount of about 40 percent.
- Royalties vary with the number of copies sold. They are figured on the publisher's net receipts—in other words, it is usually calculated on the wholesale price of the book. Typical royalty escalation figures are 10 percent on the first 7,500 copies; 12 percent on the next 7,500 to 10,000 copies, and 15 percent on all copies sold thereafter. If you're in a strong negotiating position, try to get the breaks in copies down to 5,000 instead of 7,500.
- The publisher may insist on a first option at reviewing your next book. Try to delete this provision unless you're very happy with the publisher.
- The delivery date of your completed manuscript will be specified. I usually take six months for a short book and about a year or longer for a complex one. You may have to negotiate this date with your publisher.

If there are any points to negotiate with your publisher, try to accomplish this by telephone. The mail takes too long for back-and-forth negotiations. If you and the publisher verbally agree to modify the contract, make your corrections directly on the contract with a pen and initial the additions to show that you approved them.

Signing the Contract

Sign the contract, initial any changes, have it witnessed, and mail all the copies to the publisher, who will sign it, initial the changes, and send you an official copy of the completed contract. Then it's time to go to work seriously.

Writing Your Book

Now that you've read most of this book, you know all about top-down design and bottom-up writing. More work may be needed to complete top-down design if your editor requests changes to your outline. Unless you feel strongly about certain aspects, don't spar with the editor. Editors know much more about marketing a book than you do.

Designing and writing a book is a twenty-four-hour-a-day, seven-day-a-week undertaking. I don't mean that you'll be consciously working all that time on your book; rather, your subconscious mind will continue to feed you ideas, thoughts, questions,and suggestions all the time—when you're at work, attending meetings, eating, exercising, and relaxing. So that you don't lose these gems, carry a small notebook with you at all times to jot down the ideas as they occur to you. Each day or so, add these notes to the notes you've accumulated so far. Continually expand, update, and modify your outline. Your outline and notes should continue to grow and mature virtually up to the moment that you complete the manuscript.

Preparing the Index

I strongly recommend that *you* prepare the index for your book. Publishers often hire a professional indexer to compile an index, but most indexers simply do not know which topics are important. You are the expert on your book. For excellent guidance, consult the *Chicago Manual of Style* section on indexes.

There are a number of ways to prepare an index. If you have an indexing program as part of your word processing program, use that. You'll have to compile your book into a single document and use consecutive page, figure, and table numbers. This gives you a huge document to work with, but it has to be done this way with a computerized index.

The best method is to prepare a concordance and put your computer to work to compile the basis for an index. The word processor will pick up the page numbers for your reference topics and can compile lists of your contents, illustrations, and tables. You'll probably end up with material that is about 90 percent complete. Go through the index and your lists, and spot check the entries. You'll probably have to do some manual editing, but at least the computer will have accomplished most of your work.

If your computer lacks this capability, you may have to revert to a manual method using 3- by 5-inch note cards:

1. Make a card for each reference, writing down the page numbers.
2. Separate them into twenty-six piles—one for each letter of the alphabet.

3. Use the Precedent Sort to alphabetize all the individual cards for each letter.
4. Type up, save on disk, print out, and deliver the index with the manuscript of your book.

Your editor may not opt to use your index completely, but he or she will surely use it as the basis for the final index.

Preparing Front Matter

Front matter is often the first and only part of a book that a prospective buyer or reader will peruse. It thus becomes a powerful sales tool.

The preface or introduction explains the subject, purpose, and/or plan of the book. It points out key features of the book and the audience it is intended for and sometimes summarizes the book.

Include an acknowledgments page thanking all of the people who helped, inspired, and encouraged you to write your book. This is an excellent opportunity to thank your spouse for putting up with your long hours at your computer, your kids for your being grumpy at times, and your local librarian for patiently helping you find all of the obscure references you didn't even know existed.

Mailing the Manuscript

You and your publisher should have already agreed on the number of hard copies (usually one or two) and the type of soft copy that you will deliver. The publisher needs both to correlate your disk information with your suggestions on how you designed it to be printed. I recommend that you obtain a good original printout and have photocopies made for the other copies. Keep a photocopy, and send the original (and a copy if so requested) to your publisher.

Package your treasure carefully. Use a cushioned mailing bag, and insert cardboard stiffeners to protect the floppies.

Mail it first class and insure it for some minimum to make sure it is handled properly and delivered promptly by the post office. Get a return receipt so you know that everything arrived safely.

Editing and Proofreading

The time span from the time you complete your manuscript to its publication ranges from six to twelve or more months. A lot happens over these months. First, you'll receive an edited copy of your manuscript to review and approve. Some weeks later you will receive a set of galleys complete with illustrations. Drop whatever you're doing and concentrate on reviewing the proofs *very carefully*. This isn't the time to make any major changes, since they are costly in time and money. You're going to review the proofs mostly for content, but you'll probably notice typos. Some publishers ask the author to proofread for typos, others do not. Review the illustrations carefully to make sure they've been done properly. Check the titles and numbers you assigned to the figures.

I recommend that you first give the entire text a quick reading and review the visuals to refresh your memory. When you catch any typos or errors, make a quick note and keep on reading. Your publisher may have given you some instructions on how to mark the errors, but don't be too concerned about catching all of them in this first reading.

Then go through your proofs slowly and deliberately once or twice more with your editor's hat on. Read slowly, and stop to check any spelling or grammar you're not sure of. Mark corrections right on the galleys as you have been instructed.

Postcontract Phase

Although your book is now in the hands of your publisher, your job is still not over. Your publisher is in charge of the publicity for your forthcoming book, but because of your special knowledge and expertise in your profession and your personal contacts, you can also make some excellent suggestions on how to publicize your book.

Suggest specific periodicals that publish book reviews. Positive book reviews and word of mouth are some of the most effective advertising media. Your publisher will provide a free copy to any periodical that will review your book and send you copies of any reviews. You may have to respond to some if the reviewer misunderstood some aspects of your masterpiece.

Make a few press releases yourself for your local paper and for any trade papers you think will be interested in your book.

Another excellent promotion is to adapt some of the material from your book, and write one or more articles for periodicals that deal with your profession. The article can refer readers to your book for more information on the subject—an effective, subtle, free advertisement.

If you think your book is suitable for a college text and you have included some exercise at the ends of each chapter, suggest the types of colleges that could use your text. It's your publisher's task to contact the college, sell them on the book, and provide the proper discount for the college bookstores. A college text can sell for years if the subject is not outdated.

Celebrating

If you receive any fan letters, respond to them promptly, but make sure your readers don't have your home mailing address. They can contact you through the publisher. In that way, the publisher knows that people are responding positively to your book and might be encouraged to invest a few more dollars in promoting it. Experts say that one fan letter is worth about a thousand readers since few people take the time to write to an author.

Your publisher will probably provide you with a statement about every six months showing how many copies have been sold and what money has been earned. Remember that your book must sell enough copies to pay back your advance before you receive any additional money. This may take about a year before you start receiving any royalties.

Planning Your Next Book

With your first book published, it's time to relax a bit and enjoy the fun of seeing it in print and showing it to your friends and colleagues. Your kids can share it at their "show and tell" at school.

When the glow of success has dimmed a little, start thinking about writing another book. You now know how the process works; the next time should be much easier.

There is only one way to learn how to design, write, and publish a book: go through the process. A how-to book can help you—giving you direction, easing the path through certain obstacles, and encouraging you—but in the end it's your determination that must carry you through to the end.

To me it's not the publication that is so much fun. You may feel, as I do, that publication is a bit of a letdown. To me it's not the destination but the journey to get there that makes it all worthwhile.

A Final Word

If you feel you have profited by reading this book, I'd like to hear from you. Write to me, in care of my publisher. And if you feel you haven't profited from this book, I'd still like to hear from you, along with any suggestions you have for improvement. Feedback is needed to improve any product. Any product can stand improvement.

Appendix A
Reference Sources

Abstracts and Indexes

All of the abstracts and indexes listed here, plus many more, are available on the various on-line systems.

Abstracting and Indexing Services Directory. Detroit: Gale Research, 1982– . Lists and describes abstracting journals, indexes, digests, and similar publications issued by commercial publishers, professional societies, nonprofit institutions, and government agencies. Irregular.

Abstracts and Indexes in Science and Technology. By Dolores B. Owen. 2d ed. Metuchen, N.J.: Scarecrow Press, 1985. Describes 223 abstracts and indexes as arranged in eleven subject categories, including on-line databases.

Applied Science and Technology Index. New York: H. W. Wilson, 1958– . Lists articles from over 300 English-language periodicals in applied science and technology, arranged alphabetically by subject only. An excellent source for latest articles on new, as well as old, science and technology. Published monthly except August, with quarterly and annual accumulations. From 1913 to 1957 this index was known as the *Industrial Arts Index.*

Business Periodicals Index. New York: H. W. Wilson, 1958– . Indexes by subject about 275 English-language periodicals in all fields of business, including accounting, communication, advertising, banking, management and marketing, and trade. Monthly except August; accumulated into annual volumes.

Chemical Abstracts. Columbus Ohio: American Chemical Society, 1907– . Subject and author index, known as the "key to the world's chemical literature," to abstracts from more than 14,000 periodicals in more than fifty languages. The principal source for titles and abbreviations in the physical sciences, the life sciences, and engineering. Quarterly.

Chemical Titles. Columbus, Ohio: Chemical Abstract Service, 1960– . Author and key word computer-produced index to 700 periodicals covering pure and applied chemistry and chemical engineering. Biweekly.

Computer Abstracts. London, England: Technical Information Co., 1957– . Abstracts of books, periodical articles, conference proceedings, U.S. government reports, and patents in classified arrangements. Annual and subject indexes. Monthly.

Computer and Control Abstracts: Science Abstracts, Series C. London: Institute of Electrical Engineers, and New York: Institute of Electrical and Electronics Engineers, 1898– . Author and subject indexes and abstracts of international electrotechnology literature. Separate index to bibliographies, books, reports, conference proceedings, and patents. Monthly.

Engineering Index. New York: Engineering Information, 1884– . The basic English-language abstracting service, with abstracts from over 2,700 professional and technical journals, as well as reports and proceedings published in twenty or more languages. A general index to engineering literature, arranged by subject, with an author index. Monthly, with annual accumulations.

General Science Index. New York: H. W. Wilson, 1978– . Indexes more than 100 general science periodicals not completely covered by other abstracts and indexes in astronomy, chemistry, electricity, mathematics, physics, and other related areas.

Magazine Index. Los Altos, Calif.: Information Access Co., 1976– . An automated index to about 400 general-interest magazines. Displays index on special microfilm terminal. Monthly.

New York Times Index. New York: New York Times, 1913– . Indexes all articles published in *The New York Times,* preserved on microfilm and carefully indexed by subject alphabetically. Provides brief summary of all pertinent articles, giving date of publication and page. Semimonthly.

Physics Abstracts, Science Abstracts, Series A. London: Institute of Electrical Engineers, and New York: Institute of Electrical and Electronics Engineers, 1898– . Separate index to bibliographies, books, conferences, patents, and reports. Monthly.

Public Affairs Information Service. New York: Public Affairs Information Service, 1915– . Indexes over 900 periodicals and many books, pamphlets, government documents, and special publications.

Reader's Guide to Periodical Literature. New York: H. W. Wilson, 1900– . The best-known popular periodical index. Author and subject index to general-interest periodicals (limited, however, in that it covers only about 200 of the thousands of magazines in circulation), including a few scientific periodicals published in the United States. A very useful subject index, since indexing is by author, subject, and title. From 1802 to 1906, it was titled *Poole's Index to Periodical Literature.*

Science Citation Index. Philadelphia: Philadelphia Institute for Scientific Information, 1961– . Lists the reference or coded author with his or her work for over 3,800 journals and monographic series. International. Provides access to books, papers, articles, and reports that are being cited in currently published papers.

Technical Abstracts Bulletin. Alexandria, Va.: Defense Documentation Center, 1953– . Abstracts and announces classified and unclassified or limited distribution documents produced by the Department of Defense and its contractors and acquired by the DDC.

U.S. Government Research and Development Reports. Washington, D.C.: Department of Commerce, Clearinghouse for Federal Scientific and Technical Information, 1946– . Abstracting and announcement bulletin covering reports, including progress reports of research and development under government auspices.

Wall Street Journal Index. New York: Dow Jones, 1958– . An index to articles in the *Wall Street Journal* and *Barrons'.* Subject index and company name index. Supplements issued monthly.

Almanacs

The Dow Jones–Irwin Business and Investment Almanac. Edited by Sumner Levine. Dow Jones–Irwin, 1977– . A unique compendium of up-to-the-minute information for American business professionals. An introductory business review and forecast for the year is followed by basic statistics related to all areas of business and economics. Annual.

Information Please Almanac. New York: Simon and Schuster, 1947–. More legible and easier to use than the *World Almanac*, but its coverage is not as complete.

McGraw-Hill Yearbook of Science and Technology. New York: McGraw-Hill, 1983– . Reviews the past year's works in science and technology. Supplements the *McGraw-Hill Encyclopedia of Science and Technology*. Annual.

Space Almanac. By Anthony P. Curtis. Woodsboro, Md: ARCsoft, 1989. Contains facts, figures, lists, charts, tables, and photos detailed for the general reader and space enthusiast. Looks at what is happening in space science and what is planned for the future.

World Almanac and Book of Facts. New York: World Telegram, 1868– . Often cited as the best-selling American reference work, as well as the most comprehensive almanac and most frequently useful. Annual.

Bibliographies

American Management Association. New York: American Management Association. Ten-year index of AMA publications, January 1923/January 1932–1957/1966. N.Y. Association: 1932–1967. Detailed catalog of AMA publications, arranged by subject, with author index.
—*Index of AMA Resources of the Seventies,* 1970–1976, New York: AMACOM, 1977, 162 pages.
—*Index to AMA Resources,* 1977–1981, New York: American Management Association, 1982, 184 pages.

Bibliographic Index : A Cumulative Bibliography of Bibliographies. New York: H. W. Wilson, 1938– . Alphabetical subject arrangement of separately published bibliographies, as well as bibliographies published in books and periodicals, many in foreign languages.

Business and Economics Books, 1876–1983. New York.: R. R. Bowker, 1983, 4 vols. Lists more that 143,000 titles published in the United States, organized by Library of Congress subject headings. Subject, title, and author indexes.

A World Bibliography of Bibliographies. By Alice Toomey, 1964–1974. To-

towa, N.J.: Rowman & Littlefield, 1977. 2 vols. A decennial supplement of Besterman's five-volume *A World Bibliography of Bibliographies.*

A World Bibliography of Bibliographies and of Bibliographical Catalogues, Calendars, Abstracts, Digests, Indexes and the Like. By Theodore A. Besterman. Lausanne: Societas Bibliographics, 1965–1966. 5 vols. A cumulative bibliography of bibliographies published in books and manuscripts. A massive work that is international in scope. Updated by Toomey's two-volume supplement, *A World Bibliography of Bibliographies.*

Biographies

American Men and Women of Science. New York: R. R. Bowker, 1982. 7 vols. Brief biographies of over 130,000 living U.S. and Canadian scientists, including positions held, education, and area of specialty.

Biography Index. New York: H. W. Wilson, 1947– . Name and profession index to biographical material in 1,500 periodicals and books. The most comprehensive index in the field. Arranged alphabetically by the name of the subject of the biography. Quarterly.

Chamber's Biographical Dictionary. Edited by T. O. Thorne and T. C. Collocott. New York: Hippocrene Books, 1974. A good dictionary covering the great people, living and dead, of all nations.

Current Biography. New York: H. W. Wilson, 1940– . Monthly magazine with articles about people prominent in the news in science, the arts, and industry.

Dictionary of Scientific Biography. New York: Scribner, 1970–1980. 16 vols. Covers all periods from antiquity to the present and includes only deceased scientists. Entries give place and dates of birth and death and brief summaries of each individual's contributions to science.

Who's Who in America. Chicago: Marquis, 1899– . Best-known and most useful general dictionary of contemporary biography. People included from all fields. Biennial.

Who's Who Publications: Index to All Books. Chicago: Marquis, 1990. Guide to the fifteen or so *Who's Who* books.

Who's Who in Technology. 6th ed. Edited by Am Unterburger. Detroit: Gale, 1989. Vol. 1 lists 38,000 biographies of North American men and women working in forty-six scientific and technological fields.

Vol. 2 indexes names in four categories: geographic regions, employer, technical discipline, and expertise.

World Who's Who in Technology Today. Lake Bluff, Ill.: J. Dick (a division of Research Publications), 1984, 5 vols. Covers electronics and computer science, physics and optics, chemistry and biotechnology, mechanical and civil engineering, and energy and earth sciences.

Books

Book Review Digest. New York: H. W. Wilson, 1905– . Gives digests of book reviews taken from some seventy-five American and English general-interest magazines. Arranged by title, it carries title and subject indexes.

Book Review Index. Detroit: Gale Research Co., 1965– . Lists thousands of citations of thousands of books. Author index to reviews of books in more than 450 general-interest magazines.

Books in Print. New York: R. R. Bowker, 1948– . Lists all books—new and old, hardbound and paperback—that are in print from some 3,600 publishers and that can be purchased. Author, title, and subject listings in separate volumes. Annual.

A Brief Guide to Sources of Scientific and Technical Information. By Saul Herner. Arlington, Va.: Information Resources Press. Guide to major sources of technical information; intended for engineers and scientists. Indexed.

Cumulative Book Index. New York: H. W. Wilson 1898– . Lists by subject and author books in print in the English language of general interest, including the sciences. Arranged by author, title, and subject.

Forthcoming Books. New York: R. R. Bowker, 1966– . Lists books that have just been released or are projected to be released within five months. Good for information on latest books. Bimonthly.

New Technical Books. New York: New York Public Library, 1915– . Classed subject arrangement includes contents and annotations for each book. Subject emphasis is on the pure and applied sciences—mathematics, engineering, industrial technology, and related disciplines.

Technical Book Review Index. New York: Special Libraries Association, 1935– . The best index to book reviews appearing in scientific, technical, and trade journals. Provides brief quotations from reviews. Arranged by author of book reviewed. Monthly except July and August.

Businesses

Business Firms Master Index. Edited by Jennifer Mossman and Donna Woods. Detroit: Gale, 1985. Guide to sources of information on approximately 110,000 companies in the United States, Canada, and some foreign countries. Limited to firms in the communication field.

Directory of Business and Financial Services. By Mary Grant and Riva Berleant-Schiller. New York: Special Libraries Association, 1984. For investment-oriented clientele. Cites over 1,200 publishers. Can be used as a selection guide for business and financial collections.

Directory of Corporate Affiliations: Who Owns Whom. Skokie, Ill.: National Register Pub. Co., 1968– . Cites major corporations by name and gives address, officers, divisions, subsidiaries, and locations of plants. Arranged by parent name with cross-index of "corporate children," giving name of parent company. Annual.

Directory of Foreign Manufacturers in the United States. By Jeffrey Arpan and David Ricks. Atlanta: Georgia State University Business Publications, 1985. Provides address, type of manufacture, and parent or foreign office for over 4,300 firms engaged in manufacturing, mining, and petroleum production in the United States. Access by several indexes (parent companies, state, country, and products by Standard Industrial Classification).

Reference Book of Corporate Managements. New York: Dun and Bradstreet, 1967– . Includes a listing of public relations people, with their educational backgrounds. Annual.

Exporters' Encyclopedia: World Marketing Guide. New York: Dun and Bradstreet, 1904– . In-depth information on trade regulations and practices for markets in specific countries, including shipping services, postal information, currency, and banks. Annual.

National Trade and Professional Associations of the United States. Columbia Books, 1966– . 4,600 organizations arranged by subject and indexed by title, key word, geographical location, size of budget, and executive officers. Particularly valuable for its data on annual budgets, as well as such general information as date of establishment, address, headquarters staff, size of membership, publications, and telephone number. Annual.

Sales Manager's Handbook. By Ovid Riso. Chicago: The Dartnell Corp., 1934– . A classic in the field. Each edition adds much new information on sales organization, training, methods of selling, and marketing research to assist managers. Explanation of trade practices is an important feature.

Small Business Sourcebook. Edited by John Ganly, Diane Sciattara, and Andrea Pedolsky. Detroit: Gale, 1983. Guide to information sources provided to 100 small businesses by associations, consultants, educational programs, franchises, government agencies, reference works, statisticians, suppliers, trade shows, and venture capital firms.

Standard and Poor's Register of Corporations, Directors, and Executives. New York: Standard and Poors, 1928– . 3 vols. Listings of over 45,000 companies—a "Who's Who" of American companies. Vol. 1 is an alphabetical listing by company name. Vol. 2 is a directory of executives and board members. Vol. 3 is a set of indexes to vols. 1 and 2. Annual.

Thomas' Register of American Manufacturers. New York: Thomas Publishing Company, 1906– . Massive listing that provides a comprehensive, detailed guide to the full range of products manufactured in the United States. Lists manufacturers' names and addresses, products, and trade names. Annual.

The Yellow Pages of Your Telephone Directory. Not only for your immediate city, but telephone directories of many other cities are available in your local library.

Dictionaries

General

Webster's New World Dictionary of the American Language. Abridged. New York: World, 1970.

Funk and Wagnalls New Standard Dictionary. Unabridged. New York: Funk and Wagnalls, 1964.

Oxford English Dictionary. The most authoritative dictionary of the English language. Oxford: Clarendon Press, 1933, 12 vols. and supplements.

The Random House Dictionary of the English Language. Considered an unabridged dictionary. New York: Random House, 1966.

Roget's II: The New Thesaurus. Boston: Houghton Mifflin, 1980.

Webster's Third New International Dictionary. Unabridged. Springfield, Mass.: Merriam Webster, 1961. 450,000 words and 2,600 pages. Can be used for years, even for decades.

Technology and Business

Basic Dictionary of Science. New York: Macmillan, 1966. A dictionary of 25,000 terms, followed by lists of abbreviations used in science. Lists chemical elements with their atomic weights and numbers. Written for those with little or no scientific background.

Dictionary for Accountants. By Eric Kohler. Englewood Cliffs, N.J.: Prentice-Hall, 1983. A standard work in the field, giving definitions and information on more than 2,600 terms in everyday language. Charts and forms where applicable.

Dictionary of Administration and Management. By Ivan S. Banki. Los Angeles: Los Angeles Systems Research, 1981. Contains acronyms and abbreviations, brief definitions of terms, concepts, testing, and evaluation. Also includes national and international management associations and institutions, plus bibliographic sources.

Dictionary of Computers, Data Processing, and Telecommunications. New York: Wiley, 1984. Defines some 10,000 words and phrases and has an appendix of Spanish and French equivalents.

Dictionary of Business and Economics. By Christine Ammer and Dean Ammer. New York: Free Press, 1984. Jargon-free definitions of special words and phrases used in business, plus samples of forms, as well as charts and graphs. Also lists leading economists, publications, government agencies, and laws.

IEEE Standard Dictionary of Electrical and Electronic Terms. New York: John Wiley and Sons, 1984. Excellent dictionary and an official source of definitions taken from standards of IEEE (Institute of Electrical and Electronics Engineers), ANSI (American National Standards Institute), and IEC (International Electrotechnical Commission).

McGraw-Hill Dictionary of Modern Economics. New York: McGraw-Hill, 1983. Contains over 1,425 frequently used terms related to modern economics. Each definition includes at least one bibliographical citation. Also notes 235 organizations and associations. Contains charts, tables, and diagrams; includes historical information; lists government and private agencies and nonprofit associations concerned with economics and marketing.

McGraw-Hill Dictionary of Scientific and Technical Terms. New York:

McGraw-Hill, 1984. Defines over 98,500 terms clearly and concisely with 115,000 definitions from technology and science.

The MBA's Dictionary. By Daniel Oran and Jay M. Shafritz. Reston, Va.: Reston Publishing Co., 1983. Dictionary geared to undergraduate and graduate students of business management.

Modern Business Language and Usage in Dictionary Form. By J. Harold Janis. Garden City, N.Y.: Doubleday, 1984. Defines about 3,000 words and phrases and covers usage, style, grammar, form and composition, and punctuation.

Modern Dictionary of Electronics. New York: McGraw-Hill, 1984. Provides brief descriptions of several thousand terms in current use, with pronunciation guide, and defines widely used symbols.

Thesaurus of Engineering and Scientific Terms. New York: Engineers Joint Council, 1967. Has over 20,000 entries of engineering and related scientific terms and their relationships.

Trade Names Dictionary. Detroit: Gale, 1976. 2 vols. About 194,000 entries covering almost every area of consumer interest, from appliances to drugs to hardware to toys. Each entry gives the name, a brief definition, and the source. Annual supplements are also available.

VNR Dictionary of Business and Finance. By David M. Brownstone, Irene M. Franck, and Gorton Carruth. New York: Van Nostrand Reinhold Co., 1980. Brief definitions of basic business and financial terms, numbered in order of importance.

Encyclopedias

General Interest

Academic American. Princeton, N.J.: Arete Publishing Company. 21 vols. Falls somewhere between the *World Book* and the *Britannica* in scope and depth of treatment. The full text of the encyclopedia is available on-line through a number of commercial vendors. Compact disk version is available. Intended for students in junior high, high school, and college and inquisitive adults.

Americana. Encyclopedia Americana. 30 vols. Full and scholarly; second largest. Strong on American topics, especially in science, government, business, and technology. Good, comprehensive encyclopedia for general use. Aims to be bridge between the worlds of the specialist and the general reader.

Britannica. Chicago: Encyclopedia Britannica. 32 vols. Full and scholarly, with good coverage of both British and American topics. The largest and most famous encyclopedia in English. Long, detailed articles on many and diverse subjects. Atlases in the index volume.

Colliers Encyclopedia. New York: Macmillan, 1949–1951. 24 vols. Emphasis on simple explanations. Strong in contemporary science and biography. Third in size to *Americana* and *Britannica,* but is the most current, best indexed, and easiest to read of the three. Style is popular, clear, and concise. Serves adults, college, and advanced high school students. Excellent bibliographies and study guides in the index volume.

Concise Columbia. New York: Columbia University Press, 1975. 1 vol. Capsule size for quick reference. Contains more separate entries than most other English-language encyclopedias. Covers a wide range of material found in general reference works: arts, literature, geography, life and physical sciences, and social science.

Funk and Wagnalls New Encyclopedia. New York: Funk and Wagnalls. 29 vols. Serves general family needs. Provides brief background on a wide variety of topics and is written in a clear, popular style. A useful, inexpensive choice that is well maintained.

World Book. Chicago: Field Enterprises Corp. 22 vols. Directed to an audience ranging from young people to general adult; keyed to school curricula. High-quality, best-selling encyclopedia in North America.

Business and Technical

Concise Encyclopedia of the Sciences. New York: Facts on File, 1978. Complete guide to the language and history of science and technology. Covers the most commonly used words of science and technology, along with background material.

The Dartnell Office Administration Handbook. Edited by Robert Miner and Clark W. Fetridge. Chicago: Dartnell, 1984. Chapters on management, personnel, organization of records, practices and procedures, and physical facilities. Contains a glossary and sources of information index.

Encyclopedia of Accounting Systems. Edited by Jerome Pescow. Englewood Cliffs, N.J.: Prentice-Hall, 1976. 3 vols. Illustrates, describes, and explains accounting systems for some seventy different industries, businesses, professions, and nonprofit organizations.

Encyclopedia of Computer Science and Engineering. New York: Van Nostrand Reinhold Co., 1983. 1,664 pages of descriptions of basic computer terms. 550 articles for the nonspecialist. Cross-referenced, with an excellent index.

Encyclopedia of Management. By Carl Heyel. New York: Van Nostrand Reinhold, 1982. Covers such topics as work simplification, retirement plans, and investment policy formulas. Arranged in dictionary form with a definition and explanation of the topic, its history, a list of references for further information, and cross-references.

Kirk-Othmer Encyclopedia of Chemical Technology. New York: Wiley, 1978–1984. 25 vols. Articles written by specialists; includes bibliographies. Most important reference work in the area of chemical technology. Uses International System of Units, as well as English units.

McGraw-Hill Encyclopedia of Science and Technology. New York: McGraw-Hill, 1987. 20 vols. Covers all major scientific subjects. Not too technical; easy to read. Best-known and most important encyclopedia covering the entire spectrum of science and technology. Many illustrations and some 7,700 articles by scientists and engineers. Alphabetically arranged with cross-references. Kept up-to-date by the *McGraw-Hill Yearbook of Science and Technology.*

Van Nostrand Scientific Encyclopedia. New York: Van Nostrand Reinhold, 1988. Defines terms in the physical sciences, computer technology, electrical engineering, electronics, pure and applied math, and other areas. Over 7,000 articles, arranged alphabetically, with excellent cross-references—about 45,000 entries.

Government Directories

Federal Directory. Focus is Washington, D.C. Lists federal employees by name and agency, with business address and telephone number. Includes members of Congress and details agency bureaucrats. Updated semiannually.

Guide to Popular U.S. Government Publications. Englewood, Col.: Libraries Unlimited, 1986. References 2,900 titles of government documents, most of them published since 1978, with a brief description of each document's contents.

Subject Guide to U.S. Government Reference Sources. Chicago: American Library Association, 1985. Subject index, plus a directory. Annotated bibliography of over 1,300 entries of key government documents on general topics, including science and technology.

Taylor's Encyclopedia of Government Officials. Alexandria, Va.: Includes federal and state officers. Most comprehensive resource text on public officials. Updated monthly.

U.S. Government Publications: Monthly Catalog. Washington, D.C.: U.S. Government Printing Office, 1895– . Comprehensive index listing all publications of all government departments, bureaucracies, and agencies. Gives author, title, publication data, price, and availability. Does not include classified documents. Monthly, with an annual cumulative index.

U.S. Government Reports Announcement and Index. Washington, D.C.: U.S. Department of Commerce, National Technical Information Service (NTIS), 1971– . Indexes and abstracts unclassified reports of U.S. government contractors in public and private sector. Indexed by individual and corporate author, subject, report number, and accession number. Semimonthly, with annual accumulations.

Guides

The Basic Business Library: Core Resources. Edited by Bernard S. Schlessinger. Phoenix: Oryx Press, 1983. Cumulative list of printed business reference sources for small and medium-size libraries (alphabetical entries, subject and author index), bibliography of business reference and business libraries literature, and essays on business reference sources and services.

Business Information Sources. By Lorna M. Daniells. Berkeley: University of California Press, 1985. Classic guide to information useful for businesspersons, business students, and librarians. Emphasizes current books, periodicals, newspapers, databases, and services. Gives annotated references to up-to-date sources. Detailed index, basic bibliography.

Encyclopedia of Business Information Sources. Edited by Paul Waserman. Detroit: Gale, 1983. Lists subjects of interest to business executives, researchers, scholars, and students of business. Excellent and comprehensive reference work.

Handbooks

AMA Management Handbook. Edited by William K. Fallon. New York: American Management Association, 1983. Fourteen sections with chapters contributed by about 200 specialists who analyze management issues.

Computer Dictionary and Handbook. Indianapolis: Sams, 1980. Dictionary and handbook of 22,000 terms in electronic data processing, information technology, computer sciences, and automation.

CRC Handbook of Chemistry and Physics. Boca Raton, Fla.: CRC Press, 1913– . A ready reference book of chemical and physical data; indispensable for chemists and physicists.

Handbook of Marketing Research. By Robert Ferber. New York: McGraw-Hill, 1974. Surveys the field of marketing research, including theory, behaviorial techniques, case studies, and qualtitative measurement. Arranged in some 100 chapters, with detailed index, basic tables, and additional references.

Handbook of Mathematical Tables and Formulas. By Richard S. Burington. New York: McGraw-Hill, 1973. Quick reference to many vital tables of data in math, engineering, physics, and chemistry.

Handbook of Modern Accounting. By Sidney Davidson and Roman Weil. New York: McGraw-Hill, 1983. Introduction to all aspects of the theory and practice of accounting: analysis of financial statements, budgeting, cost analyses, reporting, mergers, production costs, securities, investments, and replacement costs. Numerous definitions, illustrations, and detailed index.

People

Authors of articles. Contact the author of one or more of the publications in your field of interest that you found particularly informative. He or she will usually be happy to bring you up to date.

Magazine editors. An excellent source for information about a certain field and experts in your specialty.

People at other companies. Often even your competitors will consult with you on a problem, particularly if it's on a person-to-person (rather than a company-to-company) basis.

Librarians. They're always willing to help and can locate even the most obscure facts in books you never even dreamed existed.

Fellow employees. Check around your company; you may find an expert or two.

Periodicals

Business Periodicals Index. New York: H. W. Wilson, 1958– . Subject index to about 275 English-language periodicals in all areas of business. Arranged alphabetically by subject. Monthly except July.

Caball's Directory of Publishing Opportunities in Business Administration and Economics. By David W. E. Cabell. Beaumont, Texas: Cabell Publishing Co., 1981. Authors' guide to more than 250 English-language periodical publications. Describes types of manuscripts sought, editorial and review policies, acceptance rate, style guide, and other information.

Catalog of Scientific and Technical Periodicals (1665–1895), 2nd edition. Washington, D.C.: Smithsonian Institute, 1965. Titles of more than 8,600 pure and applied science periodicals published throughout the world, from the rise of literature to the present time.

Encyclopedia of Associations. Detroit. Gale Research Company, 1956– . 5 vols. Excellent reference listing some 18,000 national and international organizations. Includes scientific, engineering, and technical associations. Has key word, geographical, and executive index, research activities, and funding programs.

Gale Directory of Publications. (Formerly *Ayer Directory of Publications*). Detroit: Gale Research, 1989. Index of 25,000 newspapers and magazines published in the United States, Canada, and a few foreign countries.

Scientific, Engineering, and Medical Societies Publications in Print. New York: R. R. Bowker, 1980–1982. Lists publications published by 303 technical societies. Arranged alphabetically by society, with author and periodical title indexes.

Standard Periodical Directory. New York: Oxbridge, 1964/65– . The largest authoritative guide to U.S. and Canadian publications, with information on more than 65,000 publications. Alphabetical arrangement, with index of titles and subjects.

Ulrich's International Periodicals Directory. New York: R. R. Bowker, 1932– . 2 vols. Lists over 70,000 currently published periodicals from more than 120 countries. Grouped by subject, with title and subject indexes. The most comprehensive of scientific (especially scholarly) publications from around the world. Also cites the indexing or abstracting services for each periodical. A valuable reference.

Statistics

Statistical Abstracts of the United States. By the U.S. Department of Commerce, Bureau of Census. Washington, D.C.: Government Printing Office, 1879– . Probably the most important data book for all Americans. Provides statistics on virtually every topic of public interest, including industrial, social, political, economic, and cultural activities. Annual.

Appendix B
On-Line Vendors and Databases

Vendors

BRS Information Technologies
800 Westpark Drive
McLean, Virginia 22102-9980
1-800-955-0906
703-442-0900

Contains over 150 databases, is easy to use, and covers life sciences, medicine, physical and applied sciences, and engineering. BRS After Dark, a low-cost system, is available during off-hours and has over 100 databases.

Chemical Abstracts Service
Division of the American Chemical Society
2540 Olentangy River Road
P.O. Box 3012
Columbus, Ohio 43210-0012
614-447-3600
1-800-848-6538 (customer service)
1-800-848-6533 (STN search assistance desk)

Provides access to global scientific information by indexing 12,000 journals from about 150 countries, plus patents from 27 nations. The CA file has over 11 million abstracts. Specialties are bioscience and medicine, chemistry, computer science, engineering, environment and energy, materials and construction, math, physics, and patents. Graphics are available.

Compuserve Information Services
5000 Arlington Centre Boulevard
P.O. Box 20212
Columbus, Ohio 43220
614-457-8600
1-800-848-8199

Offers a variety and broad scope of nearly 500 topics and services. Has databases covering investment services; reference libraries in medicine, science, law, and other disciplines; news, weather, sports, and an encyclopedia. Services more than a half-million personal computer users. Owned by H&R Block.

Delphi
3 Blackstone Street
Cambridge, Massachusetts 02139
1-800-544-4005
617-491-3342

Covers home banking, computer periodicals, news headlines, encyclopedias, electronic messaging, business and finance, and library and computer clubs.

Dialog Information Services, Inc.
3460 Hillview Avenue
Palo Alto, California 94304
415-858-3785
1-800-3-DIALOG
(1-800-334-2564)

The largest supplier of word-oriented databases, with more than 100 million items of information stored, most of them bibliographic. Magazine and journal manuscripts can be searched and ordered on line; document delivery takes from a few days to a couple of weeks. More than 320 databases are available, including chemistry, computer technology, science and technology, and medical and biosciences. References more than 60,000 paper publications and indexes more than 700.

Dow Jones
P.O. Box 300
Princeton, New Jersey 08543-0300
609-520-4000

Owned by Dow Jones Inc., with exclusive access to the full text of the *Wall Street Journal*. Databases include financial markets, financial information, and the *Academic American Encyclopedia*.

GEnie
General Electric Information Services
401 North Washington Street
Rockville, Maryland 20850
301-340-4000
1-800-638-9636

A user-friendly service that has passed the one-million member mark. Has databases in computing and high-technology news, educational resources, financial data, and product databases. Offers a low-cost, after-hours service.

Knowledge Index
3460 Hillview Avenue
Palo Alto, California 94304
415-858-3785
1-800-334-2564

An after-hours discount service. Has seventy-five different databases, most of them bibliographic, in thirteen categories that cover chemistry, computers and electronics, medicine and drugs, and science and technology. Best for beginners. A subsidiary of Dialog.

Mead Data Central
9393 Springboro Pike
P.O. Box 933
Dayton, Ohio 45401
513-865-6800
1-800-227-4908

Offers Lexis, a full-text database for lawyers; Nexis, a full-text news service; Lexpat, which has indexed more than 750,000 patents since 1975; and Medis, which contains the full text of more than forty current medical journals and textbooks.

NEWSNET
945 Haverford Road
Bryn Mawr, Pennsylvania 19010
800-537-0808 (in Pennsylvania)
1-800-345-1301
215-527-8030

Carries about 300 "newsletters" grouped into forty different industry groups, with wide-ranging subject areas (computers, management, metals and mining, R&D, telecommunications, chemical, and energy), plus ten leading wire services. Over 65 percent of the coverage is exclusive.

Orbit Search Service
8000 Westpark Drive
McLean, Virginia 22102
703-442-0900
1-800-456-7248

A bibliographic service with over 100 databases and more than 75 million citations. Specialties include patents, materials, science, chemistry,
energy and the environment, engineering, and electronics.

Prodigy
445 Hamilton Avenue
White Plains, New York 10601
914-993-8000
1-800-822-6922

A joint effort between IBM and Sears, Prodigy offers travel help, education, bulletin boards, financial services, shopping, electronic mail, and
entertainment. It offers a flat-fee subscription.

VU/TEXT Information Services, Inc.
325 Chestnut Street, Suite 1300
Philadelphia, Pennsylvania 19106
215-574-4416
1-800-323-2940

Provides full-text versions of forty regional newspapers (thirty-six are
exclusive), plus selected articles from more than 180 regional business
journals and newspapers. Also has the twenty-volume *Academic American Encyclopedia*, with more than 32,000 articles.

H. W. Wilson Co.
950 University Avenue
Bronx, New York 10452
212-588-8400

Produces printed indexes for libraries and has about twenty bibliographic databases, including the *Readers' Guide* and *Business Periodicals
Index*.

Databases

ABI/INFORM (1971–   ). Covers over 800 international periodicals for
general business, management, personnel, and administration.

ADTRACK (1980) Indexes ads of at least one-quarter page in size from 148 popular U.S. magazines.

ADVERTISING MARKETING INTELLIGENCE (AMI) (1979–). Provides information related to advertising, marketing, media, and public relations. Includes new products, promotional programs, consumer trends, and marketing research.

AMERICAN STATISTICS INDEX (1973–). Guide to all statistical publications of the U.S. government. Produced by the Congressional Information Service.

ARTHUR D. LITTLE/ONLINE (1977–). Covers nonexclusive information sources of Arthur D. Little and its divisons and subsidiaries.

BI/DATA FORECASTS. Updates five-year economic forecasts for thirty-five countries monthly.

BLS CONSUMER PRICE INDEX. Produced by the U.S. Bureau of Labor Statistics with annual, quarterly, and monthly time series. Covers employment, hours and earnings, labor force, and producer price index.

BOOKS IN PRINT (1980–). Current books in print.

CA SEARCH (1967–). Contains all bibliographic information appearing in the printed *Chemical Abstracts*.

COMMERCE BUSINESS DAILY (1982–). Full text on-line of printed *Commerce Business Daily*, which announces products or services wanted or offered by the U.S. government.

COMPENDEX PLUS (1970–). Engineering Index is stored here monthly. Covers 4,500 journals.

DISCLOSURE II (1982–). Contains extracts from financial and administrative reports from more than 12,500 companies filing with the Securities and Exchange Commission.

DOW JONES NEWS (current). Price quotes on stock, performance of over 3,200 stocks, projected earnings per share for 2,400 companies, and other information.

DOW JONES TEXT SEARCH SERVICE (1984–). Full text of *Wall Street Journal, Barron's,* and Dow Jones News Service.

ECONOMICS ABSTRACTS INTERNATIONAL (1974–). Economic titles and abstracts.

EIS (current). Covers only current articles and publications. Two files provide information on individual manufacturing and nonmanufacturing plants in the United States. The database include sales, location, employment, industry, and size.

ELECTRONIC YELLOW PAGES (current only). Provides enhanced Yellow Pages information for the United States. Classified by Standard Industrial Classification. Areas covered include financial, professional, wholesale, manufacturing, retail, and construction.

ENCYCLOPEDIA OF ASSOCIATIONS (current). Detailed information on 75,000 organizations that are composed of volunteer members, including professional, labor, fraternal, patriotic, and hobbyists.

ERIC (1966–   ). Resources in Education (1966–   ) and Current Index to Journals in Education (1969–   ).

FEDEX (1976–   ). Compilation of *Federal Register, Congressional Record, Commerce Business Daily, Washington Post,* and others.

FIND/SVP REPORTS AND STUDIES INDEX (1977–   ). Describes over 8,000 market research reports, studies, and surveys from more than 300 U.S. and international publications.

FOREIGN TRADERS INDEX (current plus latest four years). Directory of over 140,000 firms in 130 countries that either import from the United States or state they are interested in representing U.S. exporters.

HARVARD BUSINESS REVIEW (1971–   ). Complete text of *Harvard Business Review.*

INSPEC (1969–   ). Computer and control abstracts, electrical and electronics abstracts, and physics abstracts.

INSURANCE ABSTRACTS (1979–1984). Covers literature on life, property, and liability insurance from over 100 journals.

INVESTEXT (1982–   ). Reports on worldwide companies and industries prepared by investment banking firms.

ISMEC (1973–   ). Information service in mechanical engineering.

JOURNAL OF SMALL BUSINESS MANAGEMENT. Article features and editorials on small business management and entrepreneurship.

LEGAL RESOURCE INDEX (1980–   ). Covers 750 law journals, 6 legal newspapers, and other law-related publications.

MAGAZINE INDEX (1973–   ). Indexes contents of about 500 popular magazines published in the United States and Canada.

MANAGEMENT CONTENTS (1974–   ). Indexes from cover to cover 120 U.S. and foreign periodicals in general business, management, personnel, and administration. Includes some course material.

MEDLINE (1966–   ). Index Medicus, International Nursing Index, Index to Dental Literature, Hospital Literature Index Backfiles.

METADEX (1966–   ). *Review of Metal Literature* (1966–1967), *Metal Abstracts* (1968–   ), and *Alloys Index* (1974–   ). 830,000 records.

MONTHLY CATALOG OF U.S. GOVERNMENT PUBLICATIONS (July 1976–   ).

NATIONAL TECHNICAL INFORMATION SERVICE (1964–   ). Government reports and announcements and weekly government abstracts.

NEWSEARCH (daily). Daily index of news, reviews, and information from about 3,000 major newspapers and periodicals.

NEWSNET (1981–   ). Full text of over 320 newsletters in thirty-four business categories.

NEXIS (1975–   ). Full text of selected newspapers, magazines, and U.S. and foreign news services.

P/E NEWS (Petroleum/Energy Business News Index) (1975–   ). Indexes contents of twelve major petroleum industry publications, including *Platts Oilgram News Service, National Petroleum News, Oil Gas Journal, Petroleum Intelligence Weekly,* and *Lundberg Letter.*

PREDICASTS (1972–   ). A series of files providing information on domestic and foreign companies, products, industries, markets, statistics, and forecasts.

PTS ANNUAL REPORTS ABSTRACTS (current). Extensive coverage of annual reports issued by over 4,000 publicly held and selected international corporations.

PTS PROMT (1972–   ). Information about products, markets, and company activities.

SCISEARCH (1974–   ). Science citation index, current contents to 90 percent of the world's scientific journal.

STANDARDS AND SPECIFICATIONS (1950–   ). References to U.S. Government standards and specifications.

SPIN (1975–   ). Searchable physics information notices.

STANDARD AND POORS DAILY NEWS (1979–   ). General news and financial information on publicly held U.S. companies. Annual and quarterly.

TRADE AND INDUSTRY INDEX (1981–   ). Indexes 300 trade-related periodicals cover to cover and selectively indexes about 1,200 other business periodicals.

TRADEMARKSCAN (1884–   ). Contains information on over one million active applications and trademarks requested in the U.S. Patent and Trademark Office.

TRADE OPPORTUNITIES (1976–   ). Information on export opportunities in over 120 countries.

VALUE LINE II. Updating frequency values, usually a three- to five-year projection. Data for over 1,600 major companies listed on the New York, American, and OTC exchanges.

Bibliography

Adams, James L. *The Care and Feeding of Ideas*. Reading, Mass.: Addison-Wesley, 1986.

Alley, Michael. *The Craft of Scientific Writing*. Englewood Cliffs, N.J.: Prentice-Hall, 1987.

Blicq, R. S. *Technically—Write!* Englewood Cliffs, N.J.: Prentice-Hall, 1972.

Campbell, Walter S. (Stanley Vestal). *Writing Non-Fiction*. Boston: The Writer, 1961.

The Chicago Manual of Style. Chicago: The University of Chicago Press, 1982.

Dodds, Robert H. *Writing for Technical and Business Magazines*. New York: John Wiley & Sons, 1969.

Emerson, Connie. *Write On: Target*. Cincinnati, Ohio: Writer's Digest, 1981.

Ferrarini, Elizabeth. *Infomania*. Boston: Houghton Mifflin, 1985.

Glossbrenner, Alfred. *How to Look It Up Online*. New York: St. Martin's Press, 1987.

———. *Personal Computer Communications*. New York: St. Martin's Press, 1985.

Glover, John A. *Becoming a More Creative Person*. Englewood Cliffs, N.J.: Prentice-Hall, 1980.

Gunning, Robert. *The Techniques of Clear Writing*. New York: McGraw-Hill, 1968.

Hall, Mary. *Developing Skills in Proposal Writing*. Portland, Ore.: Continuing Education Publications, 1977.

Hicks, Tyler G. *Writing for Engineering and Science*. New York: McGraw-Hill, 1961.

Helliwell, John. *Inside Information*. New York: New American Library, 1986.

Hoover, Hardy. *Essentials for the Scientific and Technical Writer*. New York: Dover, 1980.

Li, Tze-chung. *An Introduction to Online Searching*. Westport, Conn.: Greenwood Press, 1985.

Mullins, Carolyn J. *The Complete Writing Guide*. Englewood Cliffs, N.J.: Prentice-Hall, 1980.

Sherman, Theodore A., and Simon S. Johnson. *Modern Technical Writing*. Englewood Cliffs, N.J.: Prentice Hall, 1975.

Strunk, William, Jr. and E. B. White. *The Elements of Style*. 3rd ed. New York: Macmillan, 1979.

Swain, Dwight V. *Techniques of the Selling Writer*. Norman, Okla.: University of Oklahoma Press, 1965.

Tichy, H. J. *Effective Writing*. New York: John Wiley & Sons, 1966.

Turner, Barry T. *Effective Technical Writing and Speaking*. London: Business Books, 1978.

Index

259